T⸺
Wedding Book

The Complete Wedding Book

by

Vernon Heaton and Gordon Stretch

Typeset in 10½pt Times by Letterpart Limited, Reigate, Surrey.

Printed and bound in Great Britain by Cox & Wyman Ltd., Reading, Berkshire.

Clarion: published from behind no. 80 Brighton Road, Tadworth, Surrey, England. For information about our company and the other books we publish, visit our web site at www.clarion-books.co.uk

Contents

PART TWO: SPEECHES

Introduction

The vast majority of the population take the marriage vows at least once during their lifetime.

The profusion of wedding magazines and the delight with which stories of celebrity weddings are lapped up testify to the endurance of the idea of a wedding as the ultimate romantic adventure.

Yet in the midst of that romantic dream there are essential legal obligations to be fulfilled. There are also many customs that could be observed, perhaps only half remembered yet often considered vital to the success of the day!

Part One of this book is therefore designed to meet the needs of those who wish to know and follow the exact details of the formalities and the long-established customs expected of a wedding – and to give an insight into the legal requirements that must be met before a marriage can take place.

Part Two will also help anyone who may be expected to give a speech at the reception, for many grooms the most stressful part of the day! Forty-six speeches are included which could be used just as they appear (with the names changed here and there, as appropriate), or slightly adapted or they may be simply read through in order to generate ideas.

Part One
Legalities, Formalities and Customs

1
Can You Marry A Relation? The Legal Points

Certain marriages are prohibited where the couple are held to be too closely related. The Book of Common Prayer lists the forbidden marriages as follows:

A man may not marry his
mother, daughter, father's mother, mother's mother, son's daughter, daughter's daughter, sister, father's daughter, mother's daughter, wife's mother, wife's daughter, father's wife, son's wife, father's father's wife, mother's father's wife, wife's father's mother, wife's mother's mother, wife's son's daughter, wife's daughter's daughter, son's son's wife, daughter's son's wife, father's sister, mother's sister, brother's daughter or sister's daughter.

A woman may not marry her
father, son, father's father, mother's father, son's son, brother, father's son, mother's son, husband's father, husband's son, mother's husband, daughter's husband, father's mother's husband, mother's mother's husband, husband's father's father, husband's mother's father, husband's son's son, husband's daughter's son, son's daughter's husband, daughter's daughter's husband, father's brother, mother's brother, brother's son or sister's son.

The terms 'brother' and 'sister' include half-blood relationships.

The Marriage (Enabling) Act (England, Scotland & Wales) and the Matrimonial Causes (Northern Ireland) Order 1978 followed on from earlier Acts and permit a man's marriage to his deceased wife's sister, aunt or niece, deceased brother's or uncle's or nephew's widow, deceased wife's brother's daughter, deceased wife's sister's daughter, father's deceased brother's widow, mother's deceased brother's widow, deceased wife's father's sister, deceased wife's mother's sister, brother's deceased son's widow and sister's deceased son's widow.

The Marriage (Prohibited Degrees of Relationship) Act 1986 (for England, Scotland and Wales, but not Northern Ireland) allows a man to marry his mother-in-law, step-daughter, step-mother, or daughter-in-law without having to obtain a private Act of Parliament. The Act also allows a woman to marry her father-in-law, step-son, step-father, or son-in-law. However, there are certain other conditions which have to be met before the marriages can take place; in particular, for marriages between in-laws, the respective former spouses will have to have died. Marriages under this Act can take place by Licence or by a Superintendent Registrar's Certificate. They may take place in the Church of England, though not after the publication of banns.

A clergyman who may have scruples over solemnising a marriage where the degree of relationship – though now legal – is, or may have been, traditionally proscribed by ecclesiastical law, is entitled to refuse to do so, though he may, if he so wishes, allow another clergyman to use his church for the purpose. A superintendent registrar, however, must marry a couple so long as they are legally free to marry.

If either party has been married previously, he or she must produce to the superintendent registrar documentary proof of their legal ability to re-marry. Where the original partner has died, a death certificate is necessary to establish that proof, and where he or she has been divorced, the decree absolute is required. A decree *nisi* is not enough in England and Wales. (In Scotland a divorce becomes absolute as soon as it is granted.)

In England and Wales both parties to a marriage must have reached the age of 16; under the age of 18 the couple will need the consent of their parents, or guardians. Such permission must be given in writing and signed by both the minor's parents or guardians.

Where the parents or guardians are abroad their signature to the letter of consent needs to be properly witnessed, usually by a notary public or perhaps a consul.

Where there is neither a parent nor a guardian, a minor has the right to apply to the courts for permission to marry and, similarly, where he or she feels that a parent's or guardian's permission is being unreasonably refused, an application to overrule their decision can be made to the same court.

In Scotland, any two persons may marry, regardless of where they live, provided that they are both 16 years of age on the day of their marriage, that they are unmarried, that they are not related to one another in a forbidden degree, that they are not of the same sex, that they are capable of understanding the nature of a marriage ceremony and of consenting to marriage, and that the marriage would be regarded as valid in any foreign country to which either party belongs.

In all cases there must be at least two witnesses to the marriage who must be over 18 years of age (16 in Scotland). The clergyman and/or the registrar cannot act as a witness to the marriage.

2

Engagement Details

Whereas once the parent's consent would be sought before a proposal was formally put, nowadays the first they may know of it is the flash of a sparkling new ring. However, they are still entitled to some courtesy and as the odds are that they may well be paying for the wedding and reception (or meeting a considerable part of the cost) it is only right that they be informed of the decision as soon as possible.

The bride's parents should be the first to be told. (Consent would, of course, be necessary if the girl is under age.) Then follows the man's parents – and thereafter the announcement may be broadcast as widely as the couple wish.

The formality of an announcement in the press is much more rare than it used to be; most people are told as and when the couple happen to meet them. But if the announcement is made through the newspapers, it is proper to inform relatives and close friends verbally in advance. (See Chapters 11 and 12 for the wording of announcements and invitations, etc.)

The next consideration is the engagement ring, which is thought to set the seal on the betrothal of the pair and is in itself a warning to other men not to poach. Whilst the most romantic dreams often have the proposal being made by the proffering of a sparkling ring in a neat square box, many would-be grooms err on the side of caution and allow their fiancées to select a ring once the proposal has been accepted.

Though an engagement ring is still the prized possession of most girls who have 'found their man' – and remains the prized token of those who have subsequently married – its intrinsic value is perhaps less of an assurance of the man's depth of feeling today, than of the common sense of the pair who have taken into careful consideration their financial situation, prospects and intentions.

A sensible couple will have set a budget before they go shopping, bearing in mind other expenses such as a down-payment on a house or the quantity and quality of furniture, etc., that they will wish to purchase and the likely cost of any loan/hire purchase commitments they may soon be making. But however intrinsically valueless the ring, its symbolic superstition makes it almost a 'must'.

Instead of the more usual diamonds, it is common for a couple to economise by selecting a cheaper stone. Cubic zirconia or man-made diamonds are increasingly popular, and birthstones come and go in popularity with current fashion.

Birthstones are generally accepted as being for the

January girl	**Garnets** meaning	*Constancy*
February	**Amethysts**	*Sincerity*
March	**Bloodstones**	*Courage*
April	**Diamonds**	*Purity*
May	**Emeralds**	*Hope*
June	**Pearls** or **Agates**	*Health*
July	**Rubies**	*Passion*
August	**Sardonyx**	*Married happiness*
September	**Sapphires**	*Repentance*
October	**Topaz**	*A lovable nature*
November	**Opals**	*Cheerfulness*
December	**Turquoise** or **Lapis Lazuli**	*Unselfishness*

The majority of wedding rings sold are nine carat gold and when buying the engagement ring it is just as well to consider this as most brides like their rings to be the same colour! (The nine carat rings will stand up to the friction of two rubbing together better than a higher carat.) There is also a choice of white gold or platinum. In the past a plain gold band was most common but now there is a wide range of patterned rings to choose from.

In return for the engagement ring, it is usual for the girl to give her betrothed an engagement present – again, of course, limited in value to the means at her disposal after more practical matters have been considered. A gold chain or tie clip or some piece of jewellery such as a signet ring are the more usual gifts for such an occasion.

Though the engaged couple are expected from now on to be kept very busy with the arrangements for their future – the wedding itself, the reception afterwards, the honeymoon, their new home and the furniture that is needed for it (and even the trivialities of negotiations with the electricity and gas companies and so on . . .) – they still have to give some thought to their social obligations.

The engagement party is the most urgent of these and it usually takes place on the day the announcement is made in the press or shortly afterwards. It is at the party that the official announcement of the engagement is made – if it has not already been published in the press.

It is obvious that the engagement party should be held as soon as possible after the couple have agreed to marry. It would be difficult to maintain the secret for long in any event and the party loses a lot of its glamour if it is staged long after everybody knows the reason for it and all the congratulations and good wishes have been expressed.

Long engagements are often considered unnecessary, but if the wedding is to be conducted with all the trappings, on a day and time convenient to most of the guests, and a reception is to follow, a certain lapse of time is inevitable. Many couples are anxious to marry; all of them seem to prefer much the same date and reception rooms, the same honeymoon hotels and even the same photographer – which means that a good deal of planning is necessary before arrangements can be finalised.

The engagement party is usually a more informal affair and leaves the couple with a wide choice at their disposal. Again, the first consideration must be the cost, though it is quite usual for the bride's parents to pay for it, whatever the scale. However, as the same people are generally expected to have to pay for the wedding reception in due course, it can be quite a strain on them if thought isn't given to the matter from the very beginning.

The party may be held at the home of either set of parents, though, again, it is more usual to hold it at the bride's home. It is her father who makes the official announcement of the engagement.

It might be confined to a family party of, say, both sets of parents, brothers and sisters – and maybe those grandparents who are able to be there. The numbers can be increased, of course, though a lot of care must be taken in the selection. Aunts are inclined to be upset if they have been left out for a close friend and close friends are likely to be resentful if some long neglected relative is included instead of them. Tact is essential.

Of course the numbers can be expanded *ad infinitum* by hiring a hall, but many prefer to make the occasion as intimate as possible. If larger numbers are to be invited than it is possible to cater for at home, a restaurant may be a better place for the party. Everything is supplied, cooked and served – and even the bride's mother has a chance to enjoy herself.

However, even here the guests should be selected with care. It is quite usual for the young couple and their equally young friends to go on from the dinner party in the restaurant – or even from their home – perhaps to a disco or a night club afterwards. The older generation will not be expected to accompany them, nor should the parents resent being abandoned by the younger element.

The arrangements for the party in a restaurant or a hotel are quite straightforward. The hotelier or the restaurateur will advise you of exactly what you should do to make the occasion a success. He will advise on the menu, the table decorations, the seating, the wines and even on the speeches if the host is at all doubtful about the procedure.

The meal itself need not be too costly, depending, of course, on the menu, the standard of the hotel or restaurant and the style of the service. Wines will add considerably to the bill if a lot of discretion is not used. Nor is it necessary to have wines – perhaps just a sherry or port with the speeches and always, of course, fruit juice or other soft drinks. (For those who might like to spread their wings on the party there are a few suggestions for menus in Chapter 19.)

The couple will, of course, be given the place of honour at the table and if the party is given at home, they will be excused from the usual chores of serving and washing-up afterwards. The bride-to-be's parents will sit next to her while the future bridegroom's parents will find their places at his side. This will be varied at the wedding reception after they are married, where the bride will sit on her groom's left side as tradition dictates.

The only speeches that are required are two. The first will be made by the girl's father when he either announces the engagement of his daughter or wishes them both health and happiness. The future son-in-law replies on behalf of himself and his fiancée in proposing the health of their parents. The speeches are usually light-hearted as it is a happy occasion and other toasts may be drunk if the mood of the party permits.

If the younger people are to go on elsewhere or are to dance at the hotel where the engagement party has been given, a move should be made immediately after the speeches – either by the couple who will lead their friends away, or by the parents who will leave their children to their own devices, depending on whether the further entertainment is to be held there or elsewhere.

As the party is informal, dress is usually lounge suits for the men and semi-evening wear for the women. Printed invitations are unusual (unless the party is to be wide in scope) and even hand-written invitations are the exception, a telephone call being the usual thing.

Place-cards and a table plan are considered unnecessary too. Everybody knows that the engaged couple will occupy the seats of honour and that their parents will sit on either side of them. After that, the girl's father, as the host, will suggest where his guests should sit as they come to the table.

Of course, a wise host will know his guests in advance – or find out about those he does not know. This enables him to know who should sit next to whom; it could be pretty disastrous to sit old enemies next to one another! But he should still pay regard to the custom that the sexes should alternate.

Sometimes it happens that the girl and her betrothed come from far apart; maybe the man is a Londoner and his wife-to-be an Edinburgh girl. Obviously it is impossible to bring everybody who has to be at the party all the way from London, but as the hosts are the parents of the bride-to-be, the venue will almost certainly be in Scotland. In such an event the girl should try and make it possible to attend a similar party in London. This party will be entirely informal, usually at the man's home or that of his parents, and limited to those who were unable to travel north for the official party. If this is not practicable, the couple should try to bring the two sets of parents together wherever it can be arranged. At that gathering there will be no need to invite anyone else – with the possible exception of brothers, sisters and grandparents.

An engagement is a much less formal affair than it was in years gone by. It is still a contract, of course, though not in itself unbreakable without recourse to law. However, losses caused to either party through the other calling off the engagement may well become the subject of a legal wrangle. This usually takes the form of a claim for any debts incurred towards the wedding arrangements that cannot readily be cancelled (such as the reception) and for any other expenses contracted by either party in consequence of the promise of marriage.

The man may feel justified in claiming the return of the engagement ring he has bought his fiancée, and for the return of any other valuable pieces of jewellery that he may have presented to her on the understanding that she was to become his wife, especially if they are family heirlooms.

The claims of either party would only have substance, however, if it could be proved that they were incurred solely because of the wedding and represented nothing more than a financial loss because of the declared intention of one or other of them not to proceed with the marriage.

Damages for breach of promise are unlikely to succeed today and, consequently, the prospect of being able to heal a broken heart with a nice fat cheque is too remote to be worth even thinking about – and surely, to suffer a broken engagement is far, far better than to become the unwanted partner in an unhappy marriage?

3

Preliminary Requirements

Provided that the couple fulfil the legal qualifications set out in Chapter 1, they then decide on the form their marriage is to take.

Basically, they have the choice of being married:

1. In accordance with the rites of the Church of England;
2. In accordance with the rites of any other religious denomination;
3. Before a superintendent registrar in accordance with the Civil Law and without any religious service.

Church of England
Those who wish to be married according to the rites of this church will find that the venue of the marriage must be in the parish where the couple reside, or if they belong to different parishes, in the parish church of either one of them. Baptism is not a requirement for either partner unless the marriage is to take place by common or by special licence (where it is actually a requirement for the licence rather than for the marriage itself). The Church of England recognises all baptism by the pouring (not sprinkling) of, or immersion in, water, provided it is in the name of the Holy Trinity. Baptism for the sole purpose of matrimony is not encouraged, and it is recommended that adult baptism should not take place without the expectation of confirmation.

Custom decrees that weddings are solemnised in the parish church of the bride, though this is a matter of tradition and not of law. It is a convenient custom too, as apart from the symbolism of the man coming to collect his bride, it gives her a chance to say farewell to her friends if she is going elsewhere to live, and it makes the question of arrangements for the reception afterwards a simpler matter for the bride's parents.

It might happen, however, that one or other of the couple have been in the habit of worshipping in a church outside the parish in which he or she lives. In such a case the wedding may be conducted in that church so long as the party concerned has worshipped there regularly for not less than six months. This entitles the party concerned to sign the electoral roll of the parish (provided he/she is baptised), giving them the right of membership – including the right to be married there. If there are other reasons for wishing to marry in another church, a Special Licence is needed.

There are four ways in which marriage can be authorised to take place in a church of the Church of England:

(a) by Banns;
(b) by Common Licence;
(c) by Special Licence;
(d) by a Certificate issued by a superintendent registrar.

(a) The most usual procedure is by the reading of the banns on three Sundays in the parish church of each of the engaged couple, and in the parish where one of them is on the electoral roll, if this is the situation.

Naturally, an application must be made to the incumbent of the church in which the couple desire to be married. Only one of them need make the application. If the clergyman is satisfied that the couple are legally qualified to marry, he will arrange to give notice of their intention to the members of his congregation at one of the services on each of the Sundays concerned, permitting anyone who may have reason to doubt their qualifications to make an objection.

The banns must, of course, be read in the parish church of both the man and the woman, if they reside in different parishes – and they must continue to reside in their particular parishes for the whole of the three weeks during which the banns are read. They must *in addition* be read in the parish church where one or other of them is on the electoral roll if the marriage is to take place there.

The clergyman due to perform the ceremony will require a certificate from the clergyman of the parish church or churches of each of the couple if they are to marry elsewhere, certifying that the banns have in fact been published there too and that no valid objection has been received.

After the banns have been read for the three specified Sundays without any substantial objection being voiced, the marriage can be solemnised at any time between 8am and 6pm on any day thereafter, though the Church discourages weddings during Lent. However, there is a time limit of three calendar months to the effectiveness of this authority – and the banns must again be called if the wedding is still intended to take place after this time.

(b) Marriage by Common Licence is usually where the three weeks' delay taken up in the reading of the banns is, for some reason or another, not tolerable or where one or other party is not a British subject, or not an English or Welsh resident. The reasons for haste may be legion: a hurried move abroad by the groom or bride to take up a post overseas perhaps, or maybe because of family illness, or even perhaps because a birth is imminent.

Nor are residential qualifications so strict. Only one of the couple need live in the parish where the marriage is to be conducted, and he or she need only have resided in the parish for fifteen days immediately prior to the application. The other party to the marriage is not called upon to produce any residential qualification.

Alternatively, if one of the parties is entered on the church electoral roll that is sufficient qualification in itself. This is useful, for example, where one (or both) of the couple is temporarily working abroad and therefore cannot fulfil the residential qualifications but wishes to return home to get married.

The application for such a licence may be made to the incumbent of the church where it is desired to hold the wedding. If he is not able to grant the licence himself, he will be able to advise the couple of the address of the nearest Surrogate or the Diocesan Registrar for granting Marriage Licences in the Diocese.

The application must be made in person though only one of the parties to the wedding need do so; there is no need for both to go.

To be married by Common or Special Licence (see below) at least one of the couple must be baptised and neither should be divorced with a former spouse still living. Once the licence is granted the marriage must take place within three calendar months; thereafter a new application would have to be made.

(c) Marriage by Special Licence is unusual and such a licence is only issued on the authority of the Archbishop of Canterbury through the Faculty Office (see Appendix for address).

Such a licence would only be granted when a normal legal preliminary is not possible. It is required when neither of the couple has residential qualifications, or, less often, when the ceremony is to be held in a church not licensed for marriages; perhaps by a bedside in a hospital or a home where there is a serious illness – to the point of death.

(d) It is possible to obtain a certificate of authorisation for a marriage to be conducted in a church of the Church of England from a superintendent registrar but this would not be binding on the incumbent who might well insist on a Common Licence being procured or banns called.

In any event, it would seem wise to consult the clergyman of the church first – since he may find it difficult because of prior commitments to find a suitable time for the ceremony. However, if the clergyman is willing to accept such a certificate, no further legal authorisation would be needed.

Such an application needs to be made to the superintendent registrar not less than twenty-one clear days before the wedding is expected to take place and each of the parties to it must have been resident for not less than seven days in their own district immediately before the notice is entered by the registrar. At least one party should be resident in the parish where the marriage is to take place or be on the relevant church electoral roll. (If each of the couple live in different registration districts each one must give notice in their own area.)

Once the certificate has been issued it is valid for twelve calendar months; if the wedding is to take place after that time, a new application must be made to the registrar.

The cost of a superintendent registrar's certificate is dependent on whether the couple reside in the same district or in different ones. Full details of all the various fees that relate to the different ways of being married can be obtained from the local register office.

A clergyman is under a duty to ensure that a couple is prepared for marriage, and may insist that some time be spent with him discussing the Church's teaching on how people are to 'discharge aright their obligations as married persons' (in the words of canon law). Indeed, it is also becoming more and more common to find short preparation courses for those about to marry run by non-clerical bodies (see page 31).

Other Denominations

The Roman Catholic Church

A Roman Catholic may marry another Roman Catholic, a member of another Christian church, a member of another faith, or someone with no faith affiliation at all, provided that both are free to marry. 'Free to marry' means that neither partner to the proposed marriage has been married before; or that any previous marriage of one or both has been declared invalid according to the appropriate procedures of the Roman Catholic Church.

All couples marrying in a Catholic church must obtain certificates from the superintendent registrar of marriages of the district in which they will marry – the same district in which they will have fulfilled the registrar's qualification of residency. It is presumed that at least one of the partners is resident in the district where the marriage will take place. A partner who lives in another district must obtain a certificate from the registrar of the district in which he or she lives and present that to the priest. Provided that both partners live in the same registration district, only one of the parties need attend personally on the registrar.

The Roman Catholic Church does not recognise that civil divorce brings the union of marriage to an end, but acknowledges that divorce only as a legal instrument on which decisions relating to responsibilities can be made. A second marriage while a former spouse is still living is possible only if the first marriage has been judged to have been invalid according to criteria of validity established by the Roman Catholic Church. Such cases would exist when a declaration of nullity of the previous marriage had been granted to one of the persons by a Roman Catholic Marriage Tribunal, or if a previous marriage had not complied with Church Law for its validity. In these circumstances, the couple should consult their parish priest at the earliest opportunity.

If the engaged couple live in different districts, notice must be given to the superintendent registrar in both, and to establish their residential qualifications, they must each have resided in the district where his or her application is to be made for at least seven days prior to the notice being entered by the registrar. Twenty-one days thereafter the superintendent registrar will issue the required Certificates – provided that neither notice has resulted in valid objections being raised.

Where it is desired to hold the wedding ceremony within the prescribed twenty-one days after the entry of the notice, the superintendent registrar may issue a superintendent registrar's Licence together with his Certificate. This entitles the couple to marry at any time after the elapse of one clear working day after the notice has been given.

Where a superintendent registrar's Licence is sought, only one of the engaged couple need have residential qualifications, but that person must have lived for not less than fifteen days continuously in the district where the application is made, immediately prior to the notice being given to the registrar.

It is well to consult the parish priest concerning the detailed arrangements for the wedding since, although the registrar's Certificate authorises the marriage under the civil law, it does not insist that the church shall carry out the ceremony. The Roman Catholic Church still requires that banns be read in the parish church of each of the betrothed – except in the event of one of them not being a Catholic. In such a case, no banns are read. There are differing types of service to solemnise matrimony too, dependent upon whether one or other of the parties is a non-Catholic.

Generally speaking, a Catholic priest will require up to six months' notice of a projected wedding, and longer if possible. This will enable him to provide for adequate preparation of the couple. Nowadays in most Catholic churches this is regarded as essential, and not only where one of the parties is a non-Catholic.

Marriage Care (formerly the Catholic Marriage Advisory Council) help to provide 'Preparation for Marriage' courses throughout the country. These courses are arranged locally either by the parish churches or by the Marriage Care centre and information about them can be obtained either from the local church itself or the local centre. Telephone numbers of centres in England and Wales and in Scotland are held by Marriage Care (see Appendix for address and telephone number).

A couple planning a wedding in a Catholic church should check with the priest that the building is registered for marriages and whether or not an 'authorised person' will be in attendance (see under Free Churches, below). Many Roman Catholic priests are registered or authorised persons.

Free Churches

Adequate notice is also required by the ministers of the various Free Churches such as the Methodists, Baptists and the United Reformed Church (which includes most Presbyterian and Congregationalist churches) of marriages intended to be celebrated in their churches.

To comply with the civil law all marriages must take place within a church or a building registered by the Registrar General for the purpose of conducting marriage services. Such marriages must be witnessed by at least two people who have reached the age of 18 and by an 'authorised person', i.e. the registrar, his deputy or, more usually, a minister (or member) of the church who has been authorised by the Registrar General.

Many of the Free and Roman Catholic churches are registered under the Marriage Acts but some are not; most of the clergymen of these churches are 'authorised', but by no means all of them. It is obviously important to check on these points because the couple may need to arrange for a civil ceremony to take place in a register office when applying to the superintendent registrar for a certificate.

Where the building is registered but the minister performing the ceremony is not an 'authorised person', or cannot arrange for such a person to be present, the couple should inform the superintendent registrar of the need for a registrar's presence at the church. The fact that a minister is not an authorised person does not preclude him from conducting the marriage service, but it does require the attendance of some other person authorised for the area or the registrar or his deputy to oversee the legal side of the proceedings. The minister will usually be able to arrange for an authorised person to attend where he is not himself authorised or will advise when a registrar will be needed. If there is any doubt, these details should be checked with the minister of the church where the wedding is to take place.

The conditions attached to the issue of a Superintendent Registrar's Certificate or Licence are described elsewhere in this chapter and need not be repeated.

The Jewish religion

The civil law is varied in the case of a Jewish wedding to permit the ceremony to take place anywhere: in a synagogue, a private house, a hired hall, or any chosen place, whether registered for the purpose or not. There are no times specified during which the service must be held – though it is usual for the ceremony to be performed in a synagogue at any convenient time, excluding the hours between sunset on Friday and sunset the following day (Saturday), the Jewish Sabbath. Marriages do not take place, though, on any festival or intermediate days of any festival; on any Fast day; in the three weeks from the Fast of Tammuz to the Fast of Av; and certain weeks during the counting of the Omer. It is unusual for marriages to take place on the eves of Sabbaths or Festivals. For full details, consult your Rabbi or Secretary of the Synagogue.

A Quaker wedding (Religious Society of Friends)

A Quaker wedding requires, of course, the same recourse to a superintendent registrar for a Certificate or Licence, as in all cases save those of the Church of England. It requires, too, the completion of the Society's own marriage forms.

Marriage according to Quaker usage is subject to approval by their Registering Officers acting for the meeting concerned. The Registering Officer will give advice and information, and is responsible for issuing the forms and registering the marriage.

Quaker marriage is not an alternative form of marriage available to the general public but is restricted to members and those associated with them. Therefore at least one of the parties must be known to a local Quaker meeting and be in unity with the Quaker religious nature and witness.

A non-member of the Society will need to have the written support of two adult members who are satisfied that he/she is in agreement with the Quaker view of marriage.

Notice of the intended marriage is given at the close of the Sunday morning meetings where the parties are members or where they usually worship, or in the district where they live.

If no written notice of objection is received, the Registering Officer completes a form to this effect and arrangements for the wedding can then proceed.

Civil ceremony

There is no need for a marriage to be solemnised by a minister of religion. Only the civil law need be heeded and such a marriage in a register office or other approved premises, conducted by a superintendent registrar, is as completely binding in law as any conducted under the auspices of a religious body.

There are many reasons why a couple may elect to be married with a civil ceremony: they may subscribe to no religious beliefs; they may be of different denominational persuasions and prefer to marry under a neutral, secular authority; they may be debarred by the church because one or both have been divorced; the church or chapel in which they wish to hold the religious service may not be registered for marriages.

Absolute secrecy is not, of course, possible, as the intention to marry is published by an entry in the superintendent registrar's 'notice book' which is available for all to inspect. Also, all notices are exhibited on the superintendent registrar's notice board.

For such a marriage, notice must be given to the superintendent registrar in the district(s) where the couple live. Notice must be given in person and a detailed application form must be completed. The couple can be married in any register office or approved premises in England and Wales.

The person giving notice must state the names, ages and addresses of each party (with the period each has resided there), along with details of their marital status, occupation, and where the marriage is to take place. A declaration must also be made stating that there is no lawful impediment to the marriage.

If either of the parties is under 18 years of age, and marrying for the first time, the written consent of both parents or other legal guardians is required.

For marriage by Superintendent Registrar's Certificate both parties to the marriage must have lived in a registration district in England or Wales for at least seven days immediately preceding the giving of notice at the register office. If the couple live in the same registration district, only one party need give notice; if the couple live in different districts, separate notice must be made in each district. If either of the parties has been married previously, he or she will have to produce proof to the superintendent registrar, either in the form of a death certificate or a decree absolute, that there is no legal barrier to a second marriage.

If no objection is received and verified within twenty-one clear days of the entry of notice, the superintendent registrar will issue his Certificate and the marriage can be conducted as soon thereafter as is convenient.

If, for some reason or other, the couple wish to be married within the prescribed twenty-one days, they may apply to the superintendent registrar for marriage by Licence (sometimes known as 'special licence'). The conditions for its issue are similar to those required for the Certificate, except that only one of the parties must meet a residential qualification and must have lived in a registration district in England or Wales for at least fifteen days before giving notice at the register office. The second party to the marriage only needs to be a resident of, or be physically in, England or Wales on the day notice is given.

If there is no objection, the Licence for marriage will be issued after the expiry of one clear working day (excluding a Sunday, Christmas Day or Good Friday) from the entry of the notice, and the marriage can take place any time thereafter.

Once issued, a notice for marriage – by Certificate or Licence – is valid for one year. (Before 1 October 1997 it was only valid for three months.) However, if any unforeseen delays prevent the ceremony taking place as planned, the couple should check their position with the local register office for clarification.

In order for the couple to secure their choice of venue, date and time for their marriage ceremony it is usually possible for an advance (provisional) booking to be made with the superintendent registrar of the district in which they wish the ceremony to take place. Again, the register office in the district in question would be able to give more precise information in this respect. If such an advance booking is made, the couple must still remember to give formal notice to their own superintendent registrar(s) in due course in order to complete the legal formalities without which a marriage cannot take place.

Since 1995, when the 1994 Marriage Act (England and Wales) became law, civil marriage ceremonies have not been restricted to register offices. Any building approved for civil marriage can be used, and a complete list of such premises is available from the office of the Registrar General in Southport, for a fee (see Appendix for address). Any register office would be able to supply a list of local approved premises but the full list, covering the whole of England and Wales, is only available from the office of the Registrar General.

Perhaps the biggest advantage with using an approved premises other than a register office is that usually there will be more time available for the ceremony and therefore the couple will have greater freedom to personalise it. Couples can discuss the ceremony with the superintendent registrar. The legal element is the same as the register office but readings, music, etc. can be added. The only restriction is that there must be no religious element to the proceedings.

Once the venue has been chosen an appointment should be made with the register office of that district to discuss the necessary arrangements. Two registrars will need to attend the ceremony (one to conduct the ceremony and one to register the marriage), so a date should not be confirmed with the chosen venue until double checked with the relevant register office. The couple will have to apply for a Superintendent Registrar's Certificate from the district(s) where they each live and present it to the superintendent registrar in the district where the marriage is to take place, if different. (The above does not apply in Scotland, where the civil ceremony must still take place within a register office.)

While the fees for giving notice to the superintendent registrar and for the registrar's attendance at a marriage at a register office are set nationally, the fee for attendance of the superintendent registrar and registrar at a marriage in approved premises is set by the local authority. The local register office should therefore be consulted with regard to the fees for a civil wedding.

Serving members of the Royal Navy

Serving members of the Royal Navy who are sea-going are not penalised by their inability to establish residential qualifications ashore. In any such case the sailor may make application to his Captain to have the banns read aboard his ship during morning service on three successive Sundays; the banns also being read in the bride's church, where the ceremony will eventually take place, at the same time.

At the end of the qualifying period of twenty-one days, the

Captain will make an entry in his Banns of Marriage Register and issue a certificate stating that the banns have been called and that no valid objections to the marriage have been brought to his attention. This certificate must then be passed to the clergyman ashore who is to perform the wedding ceremony.

When it is intended that the marriage should take place before a superintendent registrar, or before a clergyman of a church other than one of the Church of England, the seaman should complete a form of notice in the presence of his Captain and that officer should countersign it as a witness. After twenty-one days, the Captain will issue a certificate informing the superintendent registrar that due notice was given to him by the seaman, and that no valid objection had been brought to his notice.

As soon as the bridegroom's certificate has been issued, the bride must give similar notice to the superintendent registrar in the district where she lives and where the marriage is to be conducted, and to the officiating clergyman if a church service is intended.

Marriage preparation courses

The aim of any marriage preparation course is for the engaged couple to learn more about themselves and each other. In this way they will be better prepared for marriage and for working together through the ups and downs of married life.

The content of such courses may vary according to who is running them. Clergyman will want to be sure that details of the service are clear, and that the church's teaching on marriage is understood by each of the engaged couple so that they may make their vows with conviction. However, like many of the lay courses on offer, they will probably also want to look beyond the marriage service itself to the relationship of each individual couple.

By exploring attitudes to love and sex, family, finances, work, religion, personality, communication and many other topics, a couple can discuss with an objective third party the strengths and areas for growth in their relationship. Very often these courses prompt discussion of issues that may never otherwise have been discussed. Being aware of how to discuss difficult subjects and potential problems before they arise can give a couple the means to meet and overcome troubles that occur along life's path.

It would be well worthwhile for any couple contemplating

marriage to attend a preparation course and details about courses should be available from most clergymen, or most libraries should stock the Directory of Marriage Support Services providers (which will include practitioners of the Prepare/Enrich Network UK). Alternatively the Lord Chancellor's Department at Selbourne House, London, will be able to advise where this Directory may be consulted (see Appendix for address).

4

Northern Ireland and Scotland

Marriage regulations and laws are different in Northern Ireland and Scotland.

NORTHERN IRELAND

Requirement to Give Notification of Intention to Marry

Any person marrying in Ireland, either by a religious or a civil ceremony, must give three months' notice of intention to marry to the registrar for the district in which the marriage is to take place. This is in addition to any other preliminaries which are legally required according to the particular form the marriage service is to take.

Notification of a marriage may be given in one of two ways:

(a) The couple may write jointly (or separately) to the registrar for the district in which the marriage is to be solemnised, giving the name and address of the parties to the marriage, the name of the church or place where the marriage is to take place, the date on which the marriage is to take place and the age of the parties or confirmation that the parties are over eighteen.

(b) The couple may complete and return to the registrar a pre-printed form, available from the registrar.

(If only one letter or form is sent to the registrar it must be signed by each of the couple.)

The registrar will issue each of the couple with an acknowledgement confirming the date of receipt of the notification which should be kept safely and given to the person solemnising the marriage on request.

If for some reason the provision of three months' notification of intention to marry causes difficulties, application could be made to Court for an exemption and the Court will decide whether or not the marriage should proceed. Such applications should be made through the Circuit Family Court Office or the High Court Office in the area where the marriage is to take place. One of these offices should be contacted for exact details of how to go about such an application but the procedure is an informal one. Each of the couple must make the application and may apply in person without employing the services of a solicitor. There is no charge for such an application.

The Court will expect each applicant to show that the application is justified on valid and substantive grounds and also that the granting of such an application is in the interest of the parties to the intended marriage. If the Court does not give permission the marriage cannot take place.

The minimum age for marriage in Ireland is 16 although anyone under 18 must have the written consent on a prescribed form (normally completed by both parents) or, if appropriate, an order of a court dispensing with consent. Evidence of age must be given if requested by a registrar or any person to whom an application is made for a Licence, Certificate or the publication of banns, or by the person who is to solemnise the marriage. A marriage will not be recognised as valid in Irish law if one of the parties is under 18 years of age, wherever the marriage has taken place, unless parental consent or court exemption has been granted to allow the marriage to proceed. (Applications for exemptions should be made in the same way as described above for those seeking permission to marry without giving three months' notification.)

For civil marriages and marriages according to the rites and ceremonies of any denomination other than the Roman Catholic Church, the registrar to whom notification should be given is the Registrar of Civil Marriages for the district in which the marriage is to be solemnised. For marriages according to the rites and ceremonies of the Roman Catholic Church, the registrar to whom notification should be given is the Registrar of Births, Deaths and (Roman Catholic) Marriages for the district in which the marriage is to be solemnised.

Documents and witnesses

If the couple can produce their birth certificates at the time when notice of marriage is given this is helpful to the registrar. Also, anyone who has been married previously should produce documentation or evidence of the death of the former spouse or the dissolution or annulment of the previous marriage. For marriages where one of the parties is from abroad, an official travel or identity document for that person should be produced. Photocopies of documents are not acceptable unless certified to be a true copy by the issuing authority.

At all marriages there must be present two witnesses to the marriage who must sign the marriage register. It is for the engaged couple to arrange the presence of these witnesses.

Church of Ireland

A marriage may be authorised to take place in a church of the Church of Ireland in four different ways:

(a) by Banns;
(b) by Licence;
(c) by Special Licence;
(d) by a Certificate issued by a registrar.

(a) Where both parties to the marriage are members of the Church of Ireland or other Protestant Episcopal Church, banns may be published in the church of the parish in which the parties live. (If they live in different parishes, banns must be published in both.) Seven days' notice to the minister(s) may be required and publication must be made on three Sundays or Feast days before the date of the marriage. The marriage ceremony must then take place in the church (or one of the churches) in which the banns have been published. The clergyman who is to conduct the service must be consulted about the arrangements.

(b) To obtain a Licence, one or both of the parties to the marriage must be members of the Church of Ireland or other Protestant Episcopal Church. The Licence is obtainable from a Church of Ireland licensing minister for a marriage in a church within their district. One of the parties must have resided for at least seven days in the licensing minister's district immediately before giving notice of the intended marriage. If a Licence can be granted it will be granted seven days after notice is received and the licensing minister will send copies of the notice to the clergymen of the places of worship which the parties normally attend.

Immediately before the grant of the Licence, one of the parties must make an oath or declaration which includes a clause to the effect that one of them has lived for the past fourteen days within the district attached to the church in which they intend to marry.

The name and address of a District Church of Ireland Licenser can be obtained from any Church of Ireland clergyman.

(c) A Special Licence may be granted by a Bishop of the Church of Ireland, provided one or both of the parties to the marriage are members of that church or other Protestant Episcopal Church. This authorises the marriage to take place at any time and in any place within the Bishop's diocese.

(d) A registrar's Certificate may be obtained, where one or both of the parties are members of the Church of Ireland or other Protestant Episcopal Church, authorising the marriage to take place in a church. The application for the Certificate must be made to the registrar in the district where the couple live. If they live in different registration districts a Certificate must be obtained from the registrar in each district. Whether or not they live in different districts each of the couple must have lived in their district(s) for at least seven days immediately before giving notice to the registrar. (If they live in the same district it does not matter which of the couple gives notice.) After twenty-one clear days from the date that the notice was given, the registrar may issue his Certificate. The registrar(s) must send copies of the notice of marriage to the ministers of the places of worship usually attended by the couple, and, if different from either of these, to the minister of the church where the marriage is to be held.

At least one of the parties must have resided in the district attached to the church where the marriage is to be celebrated for fourteen days immediately before the marriage.

Presbyterian Churches

Marriages according to the form and discipline of various Presbyterian bodies may take place by:

(a) **Licence;**
(b) **Special Licence;**
(c) **Banns.**

The governing bodies concerned are:

(a) The General Assembly of the Presbyterian Church in Ireland.
(b) The Remonstrant Synod of Ulster (*non-subscribing*).
(c) The Presbytery of Antrim.
(d) The Reformed Presbyterian Synod of Ireland.

Though the form and discipline may differ somewhat, the authorisation for the celebration of marriage is similar. (In the case of the Evangelical Presbyterian Church and the Free Presbyterian Church the procedure is as with *Other Denominations* set out later.)

(a) To obtain a Licence, which is the normal procedure, one or both of the parties must be of the particular Presbyterian Church involved. Application must first be made to the minister of the congregation of which one of them has been a member for at least the past month. He will then issue a certificate confirming that notice has been given which must be produced by (one of) the couple to the licensing minister. Seven days after the receipt of the certificate, the licensing minister may issue the Licence authorising the marriage. The Licence must be produced to the officiating minister before the marriage service takes place.

Immediately before the grant of the Licence, whichever of the couple gave notice to the licensing minister must make a declaration (or oath) which includes a statement to the effect that one of the parties has resided for the past fifteen days within the presbytery. (Regular connection with a congregation of the presbytery may sometimes be taken as a 'residential' qualification.)

(b) A Special Licence authorising marriage at any time or place in Ireland may be granted by the Moderator of one of the governing bodies mentioned above. One or both of the engaged couple must be a member of a congregation of the church body presided over by the Moderator granting the Special Licence.

(c) Where both parties to the marriage are members of the same Presbyterian body, banns may be published in the church or churches of which they are members. The minister(s) concerned will (each) require six days' notice and publication must be made on three Sundays before the marriage. The ceremony must take place in the church (or one of the churches) in which the banns have been published.

It is not legal to publish banns where one of the parties is a member of another church body or the wedding is to take place in the church of another body.

It must be emphasised, as indicated above, that for banns both parties must be members of the same Presbyterian denomination (not just both Presbyterians but of different church bodies) even when these are in full mutual relationship. This must be emphasised because almost all the requests that come to the ministers for the calling of banns come from other denominations, in Ireland or Britain, where this is the normal procedure.

The Roman Catholic Church
Marriages according to the rites and ceremonies of the Roman Catholic Church may be solemnised:

(a) **by Episcopal Licence;**
(b) **after publication of banns;**
(c) **by Licence;**
(d) **by a Certificate issued by a Registrar of Marriages.**

(a) and (b): Both parties must be Roman Catholic. The proceedings are regulated by the law of the Roman Catholic Church and the parties should apply to their parish priest or priests for information about the steps to be taken.

(c) For marriage by Licence, one or both of the parties must be Roman Catholic. A Licence may be obtained from a licenser appointed by a Bishop of the Roman Catholic Church. Where only one party is Roman Catholic notice must be given to the licenser seven days before the issue of the Licence and the licenser must send copies of the notice to the clergymen of the place of worship which each party regularly attends.

(d) A registrar's Certificate may authorise a marriage in a Roman Catholic church within the registration district between a Roman Catholic and a person who is not a Roman Catholic. This method is not available if both parties are Roman Catholic. Both parties must have lived in their own registration district for at least seven days immediately before giving notice to the registrar of that district. If they live in the same district, notice may be given by either party; if they live in different districts each must give notice to the registrar of their own district. The registrar(s) must send copies of the notice to the ministers of the places of worship usually attended by the couple, and to the minister of the church where the marriage is to be held (if different). After twenty-one clear days from the date that notice was given the registrar may issue his Certificate. Where notice was given in different districts a Certificate must be issued by each registrar.

Other Denominations

(including Baptists, Brethren, Congregationalists, Free Presbyterians, Methodists, Salvation Army, Jews and the Society of Friends, etc.)

Three forms of authorisation for a marriage are available to the members of other religious bodies:

(a) **by Registrar's Certificate;**
(b) **by Registrar's Licence (except for Jews and members of the Society of Friends);**
(c) **by Special Licence (in certain cases).**

(For some denominations the registrar must be present at the marriage ceremony. In such circumstances the parties are advised to agree the proposed time and date of the ceremony with the registrar well in advance before finalising their arrangements. Further information about this may be obtained from the registrar.)

(a) A registrar's Certificate may authorise a marriage in a register office, a church or other registered building in his district provided that at least one of the engaged couple lives in that district. Both parties must have lived in their own registration district(s) for at least seven days immediately before giving notice to the registrar of that district. If they live in the same district, notice may be given by either party; if they live in different districts each must give notice to the registrar of their own district. The registrar(s) must send copies of the notice to the ministers of the place of worship usually attended by each of the couple, and to the minister of the church where the marriage is to be held (if different). After twenty-one clear days from the date that notice was given the registrar may issue his Certificate. Where notice was given in different districts a Certificate must be issued by each registrar.

(b) A registrar's Licence may authorise a marriage in a register office, church or other building registered for marriages in the registration district, provided that at least one of the parties lives in that district. Under the Licence a marriage can be solemnised seven clear days after the date of notice, instead of the twenty-one clear days required under a registrar's Certificate.

If both parties reside in the same registrar's district, one must have resided there for not less than fifteen days and the other for not less than seven days immediately before notice is given to the registrar in that district. If one of the parties resides in another district, notice must be given to the registrar of each district and both parties must have lived in their respective districts for fifteen days immediately before giving notice.

The registrar(s) must send copies of the notice to the ministers of the place or worship usually attended by each of the couple, and to the minister of the church where the marriage is to be held (if different). The registrar of the district in which the marriage is to take place will require the certificate from the registrar of the other district before he will issue his Licence. Seven clear days after the giving of notice, and after administering an oath or declaration to one of the parties including a clause to the effect that one of the couple has lived within the district in which they intend to marry for fifteen days immediately prior to the grant of the Licence, the registrar may issue the Licence.

(c) Marriage by Special Licence, which may be celebrated at any time and at any place in Ireland, is an option available to Baptists, Congregationalists, Methodists and members of the Society of Friends. One or both of the engaged couple must be members of the same church as the person who grants the Special Licence. Such a Licence may be granted by the President of the Association of Baptist Churches in Ireland, the Secretary of the Conference of the Methodist Church in Ireland or the Clerk of the Yearly Meeting of the Society of Friends in Ireland.

Jews
Marriages according to the customs of Jews may take place only by registrar's certificate but need not be celebrated within the district of residence of either party.

Civil Marriages
Where a couple desire to be married without any religious ceremony, they may apply to a registrar to be married in his office. There are twenty-six District Councils in Northern

Ireland, each with its own registration office. The address of the local registrar can be found in the telephone directory under 'Registration'. The marriages must take place by the registrar's Licence or registrar's Certificate as described above under *Other Denominations*.

Registrar General's Licence

The Registrar General may issue a Licence allowing a marriage between a couple, one of whom is either house-bound or detained as a prisoner or as a patient under the Mental Health (Northern Ireland) Order 1986, to be solemnised at the residence of the person who is house-bound or detained. Notice of marriage must be given by one of the parties to the registrar of the district in which the marriage is to be solemnised. If the parties live in different districts, notice must be given to the registrar of each district. Further information about the requirements can be obtained from the registrar.

The Registrar General's Licence cannot be issued for a marriage according to the rites of the Roman Catholic Church between two persons professing the Roman Catholic religion, according to the customs of the Jews between two people professing the Jewish religion or according to the customs of the Society of Friends.

Where One of the Parties is Resident Outside Northern Ireland

In the case of a marriage pursuant to the Licence of a Church of Ireland or Presbyterian Licenser, if one party resides in Northern Ireland and fulfils the statutory conditions, that party can take all the steps necessary to obtain the Licence, and the residence of the other party is immaterial.

For a marriage in a church of the Church of Ireland in Northern Ireland, when both parties are Protestant Episcopalians and one of them resides in England or Wales, it is lawful for banns to be published in respect of the latter party in the parish or place of residence in England and Wales, banns being also duly published in the parish or district of residence of the party living in Northern Ireland.

In the case of an intended marriage in Northern Ireland for which authority from a registrar is required, and where one of the parties resides in England or Wales, the party so resident should serve notice to, and (seven days afterwards) obtain a Certificate from the superintendent registrar of the district of residence. Seven days after the issue of such a Certificate it becomes valid for the purpose of marriage in Northern Ireland. It should be given to the registrar in Northern Ireland who may issue his authority for the marriage provided that the party living in his district has also taken the necessary steps there.

If notice is given for marriage by registrar's Certificate the authority cannot be issued until twenty-one days from the date that notice was given.

Where one of the engaged couple lives in Scotland and is a member of the Church of Scotland that party may get banns read on three successive Sundays in his or her own church and receive a certificate from the minister stating that this has occurred. After seven days that certificate becomes valid for the purpose of marriage in Northern Ireland. It should be given to the registrar there who may issue his authority for the marriage provided that the party living in his district has taken the required steps there. The certificate regarding banns is not required if the marriage is to take place by Licence issued by a licensing minister or by Special Licence.

If the party living in Scotland is not a member of the Church of Scotland they would have to establish appropriate residence in Northern Ireland before notice of marriage may be given (see registrar's Certificate and registrar's Licence, above).

Where the Marriage is to Take Place in Great Britain (not Northern Ireland)

Where a marriage is to be solemnised in England or Wales by the 'certificate' procedure and one of the parties resides in Northern Ireland, the party resident in Northern Ireland should serve notice on the registrar of the district where he or she resides and obtain the registrar's Certificate for production to the superintendent registrar of the district in England or Wales where the marriage is to take place. (A registrar's Licence cannot be granted where the marriage is to take place outside Northern Ireland.) Where the marriage is intended to take place in a church of the Church of England, it is within the power of the incumbent to refuse to act upon such a Certificate, and his prior consent should accordingly be obtained. The party resident in England or Wales must also take the requisite steps there. For further information contact the General Register Office in Southport (see Appendix for address).

If the marriage is to take place in Scotland, the party resident in Northern Ireland is not required to give notice to the registrar in Northern Ireland. Neither of the parties need to have resided in Scotland before notice is given to the registrar there and notice may be given either in person or by post. It is recommended that at least six weeks before the date of the marriage enquiries should be made with the Scottish registrar in whose district the marriage is to take place. Further information about marriage in Scotland may be obtained from the General Register Office for Scotland (see Appendix for address).

SCOTLAND

There are several differences between the marriage laws of England and Wales, and Scotland:

(a) Where the banns must be read in a church of the Church of England on three successive Sundays, banns are no longer required for a religious marriage in Scotland.

(b) Residence is not a requirement but both parties to a marriage, whether religious or civil, must give at the very least fifteen days' notice before the date of the proposed marriage.

(c) In Scotland, as in the rest of the United Kingdom, the legal minimum age for marriage is 16, but parental consent is not required by law in Scotland for those under 18 years of age.

Each of the parties must complete and submit a marriage notice, which can be obtained from any registrar of births, deaths and marriages in Scotland. (The local address will be found in the telephone book.) The following documents will need to be taken or sent with the appropriate fee to the registrar for the district in which the marriage is to take place: birth certificate; copy of the decree of divorce or annulment if there has been a previous marriage (a decree nisi is not acceptable); and, for widows or widowers, the death certificate of the former spouse.

Timing is most important. The marriage notices must be submitted early enough to enable the registrar to satisfy himself that the couple are free to marry one another. He should have the notices four weeks before the marriage, but if either party has been married before, the registrar should receive the notices six weeks beforehand.

Every person giving notice has to sign a declaration that the particulars and information they have given on the marriage notice are correct. As a safeguard against bigamous marriages a subsequent check of the information is made centrally.

When he is satisfied there is no legal impediment to the marriage, the registrar will prepare a Marriage Schedule from the information given to him. This Schedule is most important – no marriage can proceed without it.

If it is to be a religious wedding the Marriage Schedule will be issued to the couple by the registrar. It cannot be issued more than seven days before the marriage and the couple will be told when to call for it. The Schedule cannot be collected by a relative or friend, it will only be issued to the prospective bride or bridegroom. The Marriage Schedule *must* be produced before the marriage ceremony to the person performing the marriage.

Immediately after the religious ceremony the Marriage Schedule must be signed by the bride and bridegroom, by the person performing the marriage and by two witnesses who are aged 16 or over. It must then be returned to the registrar within three days so that he can register the marriage.

If it is to be a civil marriage, the Marriage Schedule will not be issued to the couple but the registrar will have it at the marriage ceremony for signature. Subsequently he can register the marriage. A fee for the civil marriage is payable to the registrar in advance. After the marriage has been registered, copies of the marriage certificate can be obtained from the registrar on payment of the appropriate fee. (For advice on all fees, contact the local register office.)

Marriage via a Religious Service
A religious marriage, whether Christian or non-Christian (Jewish, Moslem, Hindu, etc.) may be solemnised only by a minister, clergyman, pastor, priest or other person entitled to do so under the Marriage (Scotland) Act 1977. Couples wishing to be married during a religious service should go and see the person who is to conduct the ceremony before completing the notice of marriage.

Civil Marriages
The procedures have been detailed in the preceding paragraphs.

One or Both Parties Live in England or Wales
If one of the parties to the marriage lives in Scotland, or both live in England or Wales but one has a parent living in Scotland,

notice of the wedding should be given to the superintendent registrar in the district in England or Wales in which one of the parties must have lived for the preceding seven days. The other party should, however, give notice in Scotland as explained earlier. The Certificate issued by the superintendent registrar in England or Wales should be sent to the registrar in Scotland where the marriage is to be held. This Certificate will obviate the need for the partner living in England or Wales to give notice in Scotland.

One Party Lives Outside the United Kingdom

If one party lives outside the United Kingdom or has lived here for less than two years, the normal procedure of giving notice to the registrar in Scotland must be followed. In addition to the documents mentioned earlier a *certificate of no impediment* will be required, issued by the competent authority (usually the civil authority) to the effect that the party concerned is free to marry. (If any document is in a language other than English, a certified translation should also be produced.) Without this certificate it may not be possible for the marriage to go ahead.

5

Marriage For Those Living Abroad, Foreigners, etc.

Marriage regulations and laws are not the same for foreigners marrying in the United Kingdom, nor do they apply in quite the same way to British subjects marrying abroad. Also, where a British subject intends to marry a foreigner – abroad or at home – there is always the matter of the couple's nationality after the marriage.

The engaged couple would be well advised to consult the various authorities. In Britain an interview should be sought with a clergyman or leader of the religious denomination involved. If there is to be no religious service, advice will be available at any superintendent registrars' office, the addresses of which may be found in a local telephone directory.

If a British subject intends to marry abroad, he or she should consult a member of the British Embassy, Legation or Consulate in the country and district where the marriage is to take place, irrespective of whether both parties are British or one of them happens to be a national of the country concerned.

Similarly, a foreigner wishing to marry in the United Kingdom, whether to a British subject or to someone of their own nationality, should consult his or her resident representative in Britain to make sure that their marriage will be accepted as legally binding in their own country.

(See also page 45 regarding marriage in Scotland.)

6

The Re-marriage Of Divorced Persons

Church of England

The Church of England expressly forbids the re-marriage of a divorced person during the lifetime of a previous partner.

A clergyman has the legal right to refuse to marry in church anyone whose previous partner is still alive, irrespective of whether the person concerned is the injured or the guilty party. Nor can he be compelled to permit such a marriage to take place in his church. Nor can he be compelled to conduct a service for anyone who has re-married under civil law. However, the clergyman also has a right under civil law to ignore Church rules and take the Marriage Service for a divorcee if he so wishes. No Common or Special Licence will be issued for such a marriage.

When the couple, one of whose marriage has previously been dissolved, is anxious to have some form of religious ceremony, most clergymen will be willing to hold a service of prayer and dedication. Although strictly speaking this service should be both quiet and private, at the discretion of the clergyman – and subject to the regulations issued by the General Synod – it can be fuller and richer although it must be made quite clear that it is *not*, in fact, a marriage service.

Roman Catholic Church

The Church of Rome does not recognise the right of the civil authorities to dissolve a marriage through divorce. In consequence, normally there can be no 're-marriage' where there is a partner surviving.

There are, however, some circumstances in which the Roman Catholic Church will not recognise the previous marriage. This will be the case when a Catholic was previously married outside the authority of the Catholic Church. It will also be verified where the Catholic authorities, in the form of the Marriage Tribunal, have declared a previous marriage to be null and void. In such cases, the Church will be prepared to marry that person – provided, of course, that he or she has the legal right in civil law by being divorced by the State from their original partner.

Free Churches

In the Free Churches the question of the re-marriage of a divorced person is very much at the discretion of each particular minister. Some of them firmly believe that the original contract is binding for life, others may accept the fact that the wronged party is being unjustly penalized and yet others will consider that everyone is entitled to another chance.

In consequence, an approach to a minister is necessary – and some couples have approached more than one minister before contacting one who is willing to marry them.

The Society of Friends

Although Quakers believe in the sanctity and life-long nature of marriage they are sympathetic to, and understanding of, those who have been divorced and wish to marry in a Friends' meeting.

Nevertheless, they are not willing to consider the question of re-marriage without all the circumstances being taken into account. The monthly meeting would need to be satisfied that the person seeking their permission was well known to them and associated with the last meeting. It is possible that the matter might be investigated by a small group of Friends so that the monthly meeting might be advised by them without the need to air all the circumstances in public.

The monthly meetings are given discretion whether or not to grant permission to those who wish to re-marry in a Friends' meeting.

Civil Re-marriages

The law of England and Wales recognises a divorced person as free to marry so long as they can produce a decree absolute. Having produced that document, a re-marriage via a civil ceremony is conducted on exactly the same conditions as those applying to a first marriage.

Divorced Persons in Scotland

The only difference between the various regulations and conditions applying for re-marriage between England and Wales and Scotland concerns the method of divorce.

In England and Wales a decree *nisi* pronounces the divorce, but neither party is free to re-marry until a decree absolute has been obtained. This is obtainable on application by the successful petitioner, six weeks after the decree *nisi*.

In Scotland there is no such thing as a preliminary pronouncement. Once the decree of divorce is pronounced the divorced person is free to take immediate steps towards re-marriage if they should so desire.

7

Other Arrangements To Be Made

In the previous chapters the couple will have discovered the procedures by which their marriage may be conducted – and have decided on the one most appropriate and suitable to themselves. All other arrangements must depend on the time, the date and the venue of the marriage itself.

The date

The date needs to be chosen with care. In the first place it must coincide with available dates and times at the venue where the wedding is to take place – church, register office or other approved premises – and, of course, with the agreement of the clergyman or registrar who will conduct the service.

In some areas it is difficult to book the arrangements because of the demand by other couples. Saturdays, for instance, are generally reserved for weeks (if not months) ahead as weekends are usually the most convenient times for the majority of the guests. Also, the couple's normal holidays from work usually need to coincide with the honeymoon so the summer months are a busy time for weddings. Easter and the Spring and August Bank Holidays are also popular periods and cause queues of wedding parties at churches, register offices and other approved premises up and down the land.

In any event there will generally need to be as little haste between the decision to marry and the wedding day itself as possible. Other arrangements might prove just as difficult to conclude, unless there is time in hand. But once the date and the time of the wedding have been fixed, the bride and groom – and, indeed, the bride's parents – can turn their attention to all the other arrangements that are so necessary to make a success of the occasion.

The Bridegroom

The bridegroom is traditionally least concerned in the making of the arrangements, though he can expect to be consulted by the bride on many matters, and to have to discuss with her some of his own plans.

Broadly, the bridegroom's tasks cover:

His 'stag party'.

The purchase of the wedding rings.

The planning and booking of everything in connection with the honeymoon – not forgetting passports, travellers' cheques and inoculations (if needed) and the car from the reception to the station or airport if they are to leave by train or air. Most couples choose their honeymoon destination together, but sometimes a groom likes to make all the arrangements himself and surprise his future wife!

The buying or hiring of his own wedding clothes.

The selection of his best man and ushers.

Before an offer is made, the bridegroom should consider carefully whether the proposed best man would be eager to accept the duty (you don't want someone who accepts only because he feels he has to) and whether he has the ability and enthusiasm to help carry out the detailed task of organising the event and of dealing with the practical tasks that arise.

Is he capable of making a speech without being a bore? Is he quick-witted enough to deal with an emergency – dropped wedding rings, the tension caused by a late arriving bride, getting to the church to find it locked because the clergyman has got his dates wrong? Is he responsible enough to safeguard the ring(s) and any other items under his charge (such as honeymoon tickets and passports)? Is he available to take part in the ceremony on the planned date? (Let him know as soon as it's fixed.) Is he totally reliable? You don't want someone who will let you down at the eleventh hour.

The final (and by no means small) consideration is

whether he gets on with the bride well enough. Although the selection of best man is no real concern of hers, obviously the groom won't want to upset her by choosing someone whom she doesn't like.

Of course, it is possible – if highly unusual – for the 'best man' to be a woman. If the groom does choose a sister or female friend he should be sure she possesses all the characteristics listed above. Also, in these circumstances it is even more important that the bride knows about, and agrees with, his choice. It is her day, after all, and she should be free to say if she cannot cope with the idea of a female best man. Of course, some of the guests may raise an eyebrow too! The photographer, minister or registrar and all the wedding party should be informed and introduced so that everyone is clear as to who is who.

The Bride and her Parents

The bride's list is much more complicated, though the responsibility for most of the items will rest on the shoulders of her parents.

She must:

Decide (with the groom) whether to be married in church, register office or other approved premises and then complete the arrangements for the wedding service, organising the Order of Service, the music and the decorations for a service in a church and perhaps in an approved premises (other than a register office).

Select her chief bridesmaid, the bridesmaids and perhaps pages, and choose their outfits.

Make out a guest list.

Organise the reception: where to hold it, the menu and the wines.

Organise the wedding cake.

Order the flowers, bouquets, buttonholes and corsages.

Order the wedding cars to the ceremony and to the reception afterwards.

Choose the invitations, have them printed, write them and send them out.

Arrange press announcements.

Book the photographer.
Arrange for the display of the wedding presents.

She will also have to buy, hire, make or borrow:

Her wedding gown and all that goes with it (to include
something old, something new, something borrowed and
something blue!).
Her trousseau.
Her going away outfit.
Her luggage.

Who Pays the Bills?

Apart from the need for consultation concerning plans and
arrangements, there must be some discussion concerning the
payment of the bills in connection with the wedding. Everything
from the decorations to the hire of the car, the wedding breakfast
and the wines, the bridesmaids' dresses, the bouquets, the photographs and even the organist's fees must be met either with a
cheque or in cash.

It is usual, but by no means obligatory, for the bride's
parents to pay for the reception, the cake and everything
concerning the celebration after the service, while the groom
meets the cost of the wedding itself (clergyman's fees, organist,
licence, etc.), the gifts for the bridesmaids and the honeymoon
afterwards.

Naturally, the scale of the marriage and its celebration afterwards must be related to the financial status of those concerned –
and where the resources of the parents differ considerably, it is
usual for the better situated to pay a full measure towards the
event. The cost to the bride's parents can be considerable and the
bridegroom's parents should bear in mind that, generally, their
own share is trivial in comparison.

Account must be taken, too, of what funds (if any) are to be
held back to help the couple to start their new life together. Of
course, many a bride is insistent that the wedding day is the high
spot in her life, never to be repeated, and she expects it to be
treated as such – and if there is anything to spare after the
celebrations, maybe she wants the honeymoon to be the talking
point of her memories for the rest of her life. Men are more
inclined to favour less publicity and pageantry than their brides,

but they are often in collusion with them concerning the scope of their honeymoon.

Other couples view the future rather differently. They realise that a large sum spent on a single day's ceremonies and jollifications plus, perhaps, a similar sum on a fortnight's honeymoon in an exotic location, might be put to more practical and permanent use. A larger down-payment on their home perhaps, less furniture on credit or HP for instance, maybe more elaborate decorations and carpeting in their new house, etc.

The Guest List

The guest list for the wedding and the reception afterwards may require careful thought. Of course the matter presents few problems where neither family has many relations or friends who could expect to be invited but in some families the numbers may well run into hundreds and even then a little forgetfulness may result in offence being taken where it was not intended.

Other couples may find that their families have a very unbalanced list of friends and relations they wish to invite to the wedding, resulting in the need for a lot of tact, common sense and maybe a certain amount of generosity.

Making bookings

All the above points need to be considered, and minds must be made up quickly if time is short before the proposed date. To get total freedom of choice, plans need to begin well in advance. Not only will there be a waiting list for available times and dates at venues for the ceremony and the reception, but almost everything else connected with a wedding is in equally urgent demand.

With holidays being booked nearly six months in advance, honeymoon reservations require equally early consideration – and attention. The printing of invitation cards can rarely be promised under a week or two, dressmaking takes a lot of time and patience, and even the wedding cake needs care if it is to be as nice as the bride would like it to be.

The photographer will have a long list of appointments, so will the car hire firm and the florist; the caterer is likely to be booked on many dates; the hairdresser may not be available at the time required unless she is given adequate notice – and even the guests may have prior engagements!

Most of the items listed above are dealt with in subsequent chapters, but everyone involved must be aware of the amount of organisation that is going to be necessary if the wedding is to be the happy day it should be.

8

The Stag Party

It has long been the custom for the prospective bridegroom to entertain his bachelor friends at a party on the night before his wedding. Traditionally, this party is viewed as the bridegroom's last 'wild fling' before he takes on the responsibilities of a married man.

But, too often, the effect on the bridegroom and the best man has been carried over to the day of the wedding. More than once in the past, because of the previous night's stag party, has a bridegroom been conducted to the wedding by his friends, hardly fit to stand alone – and certainly not sufficiently in command of his senses to be able to follow the ceremony in detail, or to make his vows in a proper spirit. The bride has found herself alone on her wedding night while her husband slept off the hangover from his stag party.

Probably with such unfortunate results in mind, it has of recent years become the practice for most prospective bridegrooms to hold their stag parties some days in advance of the wedding, instead of on the night before it, leaving time for the after-effects to wear off and for last minute arrangements for the wedding to be dealt with in an atmosphere of comparative sobriety.

A stag party is usually an informal affair, normally consisting of drinks at a local pub (or pubs). Sometimes it will include a meal. Occasionally, it will be held in a private room in a pub or in a hotel; or it may even be staged in the bridegroom's home or that of his parents (in which event the parents will, of course, be expected to go out for the evening).

It is the bridegroom's prerogative to invite only his own male friends to the stag party. As his best friend, of course, the best man will be the first to be asked (unless a female relative or friend has been invited to take on this role, in which case she should not attend this all male evening!). The others he can be expected to ask are his brothers – and, if he is wise, his bride's brothers. The actual numbers will depend on the number of friends claimed by the groom. It is generally accepted that 17 is the lower age limit, though 18 is more realistic in view of the Liquor Licensing Laws which prohibit the supplying of alcoholic beverages to anyone below that age.

Of course, the number of guests invited and the chosen entertainment – pub, club, restaurant, go-karting, etc. – will be related to the amount of money it is felt people will want to afford. It is usual for stag party guests to pay their share of the total costs and the best man should take charge of the financial details, making sure that the bill is paid (including any appropriate tip) and that he collects the shares from all the invitees. The bridegroom may decide to contribute by, for example, paying for all the pre-meal drinks (which can come to a fair sum) but if he does so the best man will make sure that all the others pay for his meal by including it in with their shares. Before deciding on any extravagant entertainment, therefore, have a thought for what the poorest guest may be able to pay and remember to warn people, in round figures, what they will be in for.

Formal invitations are quite unnecessary; a phone call or a verbal invitation when the bridegroom happens to meet his friends is sufficient. Informal dress is the norm, so the bridegroom and/or best man must make sure that everyone knows if there is any special dress requirement (perhaps ties and no trainers if a trip to a night club is planned, or sports gear, as appropriate).

The bridegroom is expected to arrive first at his party, in company with, or followed almost at once by, his best man. This allows the groom to greet his guests as they arrive while the best man dispenses, or suggests, the first round of drinks.

Of course, there will be no females among the guests and traditionally the party is restricted to unmarried men; however, most people nowadays ignore the second restriction – and as it is the bridegroom's party, who can deny him the right to stretch convention as much as he likes?

The main speech of the evening is expected to be made by the best man. If the evening includes a meal, then the best man will probably be sitting at the foot of the table and will make his speech at the coffee stage.

The speech should be entertaining, humorous, full of happy stories, and slanted to poke as much fun as possible at the bridegroom. Unless he is extremely quick-witted with an unusually fast-moving mind, the best man should prepare the text of his speech in advance and, if necessary, rehearse it to the point where it sounds 'off the cuff' and unrehearsed.

The contents must be amusing, anecdotal and entirely concerned with the bridegroom and his friends. However, it should not be too long or the listeners will get bored.

The best man may make use of his personal knowledge of the groom and refer to:

An event or two which took place during their schooldays;

The unfortunate girls – unnamed – that are now to be abandoned by the bridegroom . . . and the difficulties in getting rid of them;

The idea that two can live as cheaply as one being a fallacy;

Some of the means whereby he can escape his fate: the river, the French Foreign Legion, a Trappist Monastery or a slow boat to the East.

The bridegroom responds with an equally farcical farewell to his 'bachelor' friends – friends whom he is glad to abandon because of their shockingly selfish way of life; a bunch of reprobates, boozers and ill-mannered oafs.

The bridegroom can include in his speech, humorously:

A sad farewell to his past girlfriends.

A welcome at his home for all his male friends – so long as they wipe their shoes on the doormat.

A request that financial aid should not be withheld if they ever again meet in a pub.

An entertainment is not really necessary at such a party. However, if there is one it should be confined to a single act, e.g. a comedian. A female entertainer may be engaged, *but only* if the bride is not likely to be upset to hear about it.

The bridegroom should be the last to leave the party – usually in company with his best man and, if necessary, by taxi. The best man should be in a fit state to make sure that anyone driving home from the party is fully sober.

9

The Hen Party

Not to be out-done, the bride often organises her own celebration with her chief bridesmaid, sisters (both hers and the groom's, if appropriate) and female friends. (The bridesmaids may be included, too, if they are not too young.) This is often a quieter event than the groom's Stag Party – although not always!

The way in which a Hen Party is celebrated is entirely up to the bride. For example, many choose to go to a pub and/or club, others arrange a meal in a restaurant or at home, while yet others may opt for an evening (or perhaps a day) at a health club for a spot of pampering.

Invitation is usually by word of mouth and it should be made clear to anyone invited what the plan for the evening is, so they can dress appropriately and know what the likely cost is to be. A thought should be spared for the poorest in the group during the organising of the evening and nothing planned that will over-stretch such pockets.

A sensible bride will organise her Hen Party to take place well before her wedding. Last minute arrangements may well take up most of her time on the day before the wedding, so she'll need to be clear-headed for them, and on the evening before her big day she will want to be able to take a break from all the bustle of preparation and have time to relax (as much as she can!).

10

Who Does What?

One of the earliest tasks of the bride and the bridegroom is to choose who are to be their helpers before, during and immediately after their wedding.

The matter needs careful thought if jealousies are not to be aroused. Relations often feel that they have a claim to be more than guests at a wedding; long-standing friends expect similar privileges – and not one of them may be suited to the particular duties involved.

Possibly he who considers himself most entitled to the office of best man is debarred because he has too little time to spare before the wedding, perhaps because he knows so few of the people concerned and would, in consequence, make a poor marshal, and not improbably because, however sincere he may be, he may lack the flair for organisation, the capacity to take charge of a situation, or not be quick-witted enough to deal with an emergency.

Equally, an 'anxious-to-be' bridesmaid may not be led to understand that she is the 'one-too-many' of the girls who can hope to be invited to join the bridal procession. Maybe, too, her lack of composure would be likely to cause embarrassment during the ceremony, or possibly she has been excluded because her ability to remain standing on her feet throughout the service is in doubt – or even because her height just cannot be matched to that of any other suitable girl.

Others, of course, have duties which are inescapable. The need for the bride's father to be present at the church to give her away, for instance, is almost obligatory. Only where he is dead, physically incapable of attending the service or estranged from the family should a deputy be appointed.

The Chief Bridesmaid

It is quite usual for the bride to seek the help of her eldest unmarried sister as her chief bridesmaid, or, if she has no sister, another unmarried relative or her best unmarried friend.

There is no bounden duty laid on the bride to make such a choice if she considers another unmarried relative or friend temperamentally more suitable – but the alternative selection should not be made lightly and the unmarried sister or best friend who has been passed over should be told by the bride herself the reason for her decision, in the hope that goodwill and harmony will not be jeopardized.

The chief bridesmaid's duties are concerned mainly with two things: personal attention to the bride, and the marshalling of the bridesmaids and pages.

She might be expected to help the bride to choose the bridesmaids' dresses, to rehearse them in their duties and to take charge of the bride's bouquet during the service.

She might be called upon to help dress the bride for her wedding, though this task is usually claimed by the bride's mother as a last service to her daughter. In any event, the chief bridesmaid will have enough to do to dress herself and to see to it that the bridesmaids are properly dressed for the occasion; their head-dresses, their posies, their shoes and the correct hang of their dresses – not to mention their arrival at the church well in advance of the bride.

During the service, the chief bridesmaid's station is immediately behind the bride and the bride's father. She will follow them in procession to the chancel steps or to the registrar and then, passing her own bouquet to the nearest bridesmaid, she will take the bridal bouquet and draw the bride's veil clear of her face.

If the service is held in a church, when the newly-wed couple follow the clergyman into the vestry for the formality of signing the register, she and the best man follow immediately behind them.

Often the chief bridesmaid (if she is of age) and the best man are chosen to sign the register as witnesses to the marriage.

The chief bridesmaid should be available to the bride during the reception, to smooth away any little worries or difficulties that may arise – often in consultation with the best man. Her final duty is to help the bride into her 'going away' outfit if she is needed, and to see her to the car.

The Bridesmaids

The bridesmaids are chosen by the bride from amongst her young friends and relatives or those of the bridegroom. They generally number two or four, though for high-profile weddings the numbers may rise as high as six or even eight. The bride's attendants need not all be girls; young boys may be included as pages. Pages are always very young – 5 to 8 years of age are the most acceptable limits, although there is nothing mandatory about it. They are nearly always young brothers or nephews of the couple.

It is worth remembering that while very small bridesmaids and pages may look adorable, they are going to find standing still without talking during the service very difficult, and it is common sense to choose children of an age that can understand what is required and what is going on.

A bride almost always tries to match the bridesmaids and pages for size, sometimes a difficult task but making a most attractive picture when she has been successful. It is the bride's prerogative, too, to choose the material and pattern for the bridesmaids' dresses and the pages' outfits, and any accessories to be worn and bouquets etc. to be carried.

By tradition, the mothers of the bridesmaids each pay for their daughter's attire – an expensive business if the bride's choice happens to be ambitious. Hopefully they will be used as party dresses afterwards.

The bride should take care not to invite anyone to act as her bridesmaid whose parents would be unlikely to welcome the expense – unless, as is sometimes the case, the bride's parents will provide the whole of the ensemble for each of the bridesmaids. Whoever pays for the dresses and accessories, it is usual to allow the bridesmaids to keep them after the wedding unless they are hired.

Most large department stores have a bridal department where there is a wide range of bridal gowns, veils, head dresses and bridesmaids' dresses to choose from. Alternatively, a good dressmaker could prove of immense help in deciding on the ensemble; she will advise, too, on what is suitable for the time of the year, the fashionable styles, and have a sense of matching colours and of trimmings that will enhance the group as a whole. She will be able to make suggestions concerning the modern trend in headdresses, be that hats, tiaras, circlets or bows. She will know whether or not a veil should be worn by the bride and even be able to advise on the most suitable posies or flower baskets to match or contrast with the dresses. There are also plenty of bridal magazines on the market which are full of current trends and ideas.

The duty of the bridesmaids and pages is to assist the bride from the moment she arrives at the venue for her wedding until she finally leaves the reception on the first stage of her honeymoon. 'Assist' is hardly the word as far as the wedding ceremony is concerned; the bridesmaids and pages are merely decorative in the procession and have no duty other than to attend to the bridal train – if it should be long enough to require attention. In the procession they follow in pairs behind the bride, the pages leading and the taller or older bridesmaids coming last.

At the reception afterwards, the bridesmaids might be expected to take round portions of the wedding cake, at the proper time, and offer them to the guests – but after that their duties are complete and they can enjoy themselves for the rest of the day as each of them sees fit.

Matron of Honour

There is no absolute need for a bride to be attended by a retinue of bridesmaids. Sometimes it may be that she has no young female relatives or, indeed, any suitable young friends available. This often happens if the bride is new to the district, or has travelled some considerable distance to marry.

Sometimes, too, the bride may be older and young bridesmaids may be out of place; or it may even be that she is most anxious to ask some particular woman to attend her who happens to be married, especially a sister.

In all such cases it is quite usual for the bride to be attended by a matron of honour. The lady chosen will be a married woman and she will be the only attendant, acting as the chief – and only – bridesmaid.

Her duties are identical with those of a chief bridesmaid, but she will not wear the finery. The bride, too, usually abandons the full wedding dress and veil for an outfit similar to that worn by her matron of honour – though this is by no means a must.

The Bride's Mother

The bride's mother is one of those who have inescapable duties to perform in connection with her daughter's wedding – unless she happens to be incapacitated, when her mantle will fall on the bride's oldest sister if she has one, or an aunt or even a grandmother.

Yet, despite the fact that she will probably have to work harder than anyone else to make for the success of the occasion, the bride's mother will have almost no official part in the wedding itself.

She will carry the whole of the responsibility for the social side of the event and as the hostess she will issue the invitations to the wedding guests both to the ceremony and to the reception afterwards. She will need to exercise a great deal of tact, too, to include as far as possible the guests suggested by the bridegroom's parents, bearing in mind that she and her husband will be expected to pay the bills!

The bride's mother will be deeply concerned in helping to choose the bridal gown and no doubt her advice will be sought concerning the bridesmaid's dresses.

Among the other cares she must shoulder, in consultation with the bride, are:

1. The choosing, printing and despatching of the invitations.
2. The press announcements.
3. The printing of the Order of Service as arranged between the couple and the clergyman or registrar.
4. The decorations for the venue of the ceremony.
5. The wedding bouquets, buttonholes and corsages for the two mothers – in consultation with the bride to make sure that they are all in harmony.
6. Ordering the wedding cars to take the bride and her father, the bridesmaids, and of course herself, to the ceremony. She may also need to order cars wanted by other guests – and to make arrangements to get everybody from the ceremony to the reception afterwards. The only cars that will not require her attention are those that will carry the bridegroom and his best man to the ceremony and the 'going away' car for the bridal couple on the first stage of their honeymoon, which the bridegroom should arrange.
7. She will have to make and ice (or have made and iced) the wedding cake and arrange for its delivery to the reception venue.
8. The photographer needs to be booked. He will normally take photographs of the bride arriving with her father for the

ceremony and may, if asked, go to the bride's house before the wedding party depart for the ceremony to take a few photographs there. Sometimes he is allowed to take photographs during parts of the service or during the signing of the register, but most photographs will be of the bride and groom with their bridesmaids and pages, their parents and other relatives after the ceremony is finished. The photographer will, if the couple wish, take some black and white shots and, together with a form which includes all the relevant details and will have been completed by the bride and groom, send one to the local newspaper who will print it free of charge at the editor's discretion. The photographer will also arrive at the reception before the guests to take the 'official' and 'pretend' photograph of the cutting of the cake. The cake usually has several tiers and this may be the only time to photograph it complete, as many caterers take away the middle tier to cut it up during the reception. There will be plenty of amateur photographers around to capture the actual moment of the cutting of the cake.

9. Arranging for a video recording to be taken of the ceremony, and perhaps the celebrations afterwards, with the approval of the clergyman or registrar conducting the ceremony.

10. Arranging the details of the reception in consultation with the caterer and arranging where this is to be held, including:
    (a) the menu
    (b) the wines
    (c) the table decorations
    (d) the seating arrangements
    (e) booking a private room for the bride where she can change into her 'going away' outfit
    (f) drawing up a table plan if needed
    (g) arranging the printing of place cards, menus, book matches, table napkins, as desired.

11. The collection of what is left of the wedding cake after the reception; the cutting and boxing of the portions for posting to distant relatives and friends.

(There are some firms who will take on everything for the bride's mother, from catering to car hire, flowers, photography, video recording, the wedding cake, entertainment, stationery, bridal wear and hire facilities.)

As the wedding will, in all probability, take place in the district of the bride's family home, her mother can expect to do some entertaining in addition to the gathering of friends and relatives at the reception. This will be particularly strenuous if the bridegroom, his family and friends come from any considerable distance.

As the hostess, the bride's mother may find herself involved in arranging hotel accommodation for some of the guests and may even feel duty bound to put some of the bridegroom's relatives up in her own home. She should be aware, however, that on the day of the wedding itself it may cause difficulties if there are too many people in the house. It should be remembered that the bridesmaids will be meeting there to get ready for the wedding, the photographer may well come round before the wedding to take pictures of the bride at home and there will be bustle enough without the addition of overnight guests.

She will also find that her daughter will need her help in dressing for the wedding. Although it is the duty of the chief bridesmaid to attend the bride, few mothers are willing to forego this last chore for their daughters. She will then leave the bride at home with her father and make haste, either alone or with the bridesmaids, to reach the church or civil venue ahead of her.

Her place during the marriage service is in the front row of the pews on the bride's side of the aisle, to the left facing the altar for a church wedding, or the front seats in a civil ceremony, among her other children and perhaps her parents.

She takes no part in the ceremony, although if it is a church wedding she will be led by the bridegroom's father to the vestry (perhaps as a witness to the signing of the marriage register). She comes out of the church on the left arm of the bridegroom's father following the pages and bridesmaids in procession, with the bridegroom's mother and the bride's father behind them.

She and her husband should leave for the reception immediately after the newly-weds. They are the hosts and must, of course, be there first, in time to receive their guests.

The Bride's Father

The bride's father has the dual privilege of giving his daughter away at her wedding – and paying for the reception afterwards.

Attired in morning dress or lounge suit (to match the rest of the men in the wedding party), and wearing a buttonhole similar to that worn by the bridegroom and the best man, the bride's father escorts his daughter from their home to the ceremony. If for any reason her father is unable to attend the wedding, the bride's eldest brother, uncle or male guardian usually takes his place (although, of course, there is no reason why her mother cannot give her away, if the bride so desires – and the mother agrees).

He arrives at the venue for the ceremony with the bride after everyone else has gathered within, though it is bad form to keep everyone waiting after the appointed time. Almost at once, with his daughter on his right arm, he will lead the procession towards the chancel steps or other agreed place, as appropriate (depending on whether the ceremony is to take place in a church or in a building registered for civil marriages). At a register office the guests will often be waiting outside and the wedding party all enter the building together.

At the proper time in the church service, he will take his daughter's hand and give it to the clergyman in a gesture of giving her away. (This is not a part of the civil ceremony.) After the service, the bride's father accompanies the bridegroom's mother into the vestry in the wake of the newly-weds, to see the final act of the marriage – the signing of the register.

Immediately after leaving the ceremony he will hurry with his wife to the venue of the reception where, as host and hostess, they greet their guests.

Finally, the bride's father will be called on by the best man, during the reception, to propose the toast of the 'Bride and Bridegroom'.

The Best Man
The best man is chosen by the bridegroom from amongst his relatives or friends. He is traditionally unmarried, although, in general, it is the groom's closest companion that is honoured. (He might also, in very rare circumstances, be a she – see page 52.)

The duties are onerous and the bridegroom would be well advised to make his selection with extreme care. The best man will find himself a sort of master of ceremonies, the chief usher, the repository of valuables – such as the wedding ring(s) and the certificate permitting the marriage – organiser-in-chief, toastmaster and paymaster. He is also likely to find himself the bridegroom's messenger boy, father confessor, persuader, remembrance, office boy and valet.

Obviously he must have a flair for organisation, a steady nerve, be a good mixer and have limitless tact. His many duties include:

1. Getting the bridegroom to his wedding – on time. (He should talk to the groom in advance of the day to establish the arrangements for getting himself and the groom to the ceremony.)
2. Detailing the ushers to their duties.
3. Safeguarding the wedding ring(s) until exchanged by the couple.
4. After the service, accompanying the chief bridesmaid to the vestry, if appropriate, behind the bride and bridegroom.
5. Possibly to act as a witness to the signing of the register, often with the chief bridesmaid. (The bride and groom may, of course, choose other witnesses and, to avoid confusion at the very last moment, it is well that it be decided and confirmed who the official witnesses are to be well in advance.)
6. He should follow the bride and groom out of the ceremony with the chief bridesmaid and then be at the door to usher the newly-weds to their places in front of the photographer and see them to their car for the journey to the reception. He then ushers the guests into their cars in turn – parents first, grandparents, uncles and aunts, bridesmaids and then the friends and more distant relatives.
7. He pays the marriage fees as appropriate (possibly including the cost of the organist, the choir and bells) if this has not already been done.
8. At the reception he calls on the speakers and replies to the toast of 'The Bridesmaids' on their behalf.
9. He reads out any messages of congratulations that have been received.
10. He sees the couple into their car or taxi after the reception (which he may have to organise – another detail to check well in advance of the wedding day), ready for the start of their honeymoon journey, hands over the various documents such as rail or air tickets, passports, traveller's cheques, route maps and perhaps luggage which he may have been safe-guarding during the ceremony and the reception.

Though the best man is traditionally supposed to help the bridegroom to dress for his wedding, this is hardly necessary with modern clothes. In the picturesque days of the Prince Regent, of course, with the magnificent velvets, silks and satins, socks, stockings and shoe buckles worn by the bridegrooms, the best man needed the services of a valet to help him dress the nervous buck – and many an hour to spare for the purpose!

Today, the best man usually arrives at the bridegroom's home as the latter is dressing, collects the wedding ring(s), identifies the baggage, takes charge of the keys, the various tickets and other documents needed for the honeymoon and the cash necessary to pay any outstanding marriage fees – in other words, generally checks that nothing has been forgotten. Even then he will probably find that the nervous bridegroom has neglected to provide himself with a pair of black socks or has broken a shoelace and there isn't a spare!

Once he and the bridegroom are ready there is nothing for it but to watch the clock and worry about getting to the ceremony in good time. Nothing could make a more embarrassing start to a wedding than for the bridegroom to arrive at the ceremony after his bride! From then on he continually fingers the ring(s) in his waistcoat pocket, knowing that though he would be by no means the first best man to forget it, his failure to produce it at the right moment might constitute a disaster.

The best man's clothes are similar to those worn by the bridegroom. If it is a very formal wedding and the groom is wearing morning dress, then the best man would wear the same. For less formal weddings the groom and best man wear lounge suits, often matching ones. (The female best man should also be readily identifiable in her role and a formal skirt suit with a buttonhole to match that of the groom would be most appropriate.)

Whatever the type of wedding, the bridegroom and best man wear buttonholes, which the best man should collect unless they are being delivered straight to the groom's house. It is usual for the groom and best man and the two fathers to have the same buttonholes – white, red, pink or yellow carnations or roses – while the ushers all have white or red buttonholes. But it is equally possible for the groom to have a buttonhole to harmonise with his suit. The choice is usually the bride's who will order all the flowers with her mother.

Ushers or 'Groomsmen'

When appointing ushers, the bridegroom (generally in consultation with his best man and often the bride) must take into account family 'considerations'. It is usual to make the choice from the unmarried brothers and friends of both the bridegroom and his bride, and a great deal of tact needs to be exercised if somebody is not going to protest: 'If you ask *him* you can't leave out *so-and-so*'. It is important that each side should be represented in order that as many of the guests as possible will be recognised and received by name.

The number of ushers required will depend largely on the number of people who are invited to the ceremony. If less than fifty or sixty guests are invited, then only two ushers are generally needed. A further two ushers could well be needed to cope with each additional fifty/sixty guests, though there is no hard and fast ruling on the matter. The need is to have sufficient ushers to receive the guests, hand them Order of Service sheets (if appropriate) and conduct them to their places for the ceremony.

The ushers must, of course, arrive first at the venue for the ceremony to greet the guests as they appear. It is quite correct for an usher to meet a guest in the entrance and ask 'Friend of the bride, or of the groom?', in order to determine on which side they should sit, but it is much more welcoming to receive them by name and, thus, know to which side they should be conducted. Tradition dictates that relatives and friends of the bride sit on the left of the aisle facing the chancel steps or the place where the ceremony will take place, and those of the bridegroom on the right – the immediate families of the bride and bridegroom being placed in the front rows on their respective sides. This system would work just as well at a civil venue if it is possible to organise the seating in this way (although register offices are often limited in space).

Dress for the ushers should be similar to that worn by the bridegroom and best man: morning dress or dark lounge suits. Buttonholes, usually of carnations, are worn in their coat lapels.

During the ceremony the ushers should sit near the back in order to be in a convenient position to deal with any late-comers and to open the doors for the bridal party to process out, if appropriate.

Chief usher

If the best man lives far from the bridegroom or, because of circumstances, is able to travel to the venue of the wedding and stay there for just a few days (or perhaps only the day of the wedding itself) it may be advisable to appoint a chief usher or 'deputy best man'.

The choice of such an individual should be made by consultation between the bridegroom and the best man, bearing in mind that:

(a) he must be willing, capable and have the time to act as deputy to the best man during probably the whole of the preliminaries;

(b) he must be a friend of the bridegroom as they will be involved together making the arrangements and carrying out the practical details;

(c) he must be a close friend of the best man who will expect him to have ready, and be able to turn over to him with the shortest of briefings, all the information and items he will require for the wedding.

The duties of chief usher are, of course, those of the best man, up to and until the best man is available to take over for himself.

However, in his role as usher his most important duty is to take responsibility for greeting the mother of the bride when she arrives and conduct her to the front left-hand pew or row of seats.

11

Announcements

The first public proclamation of the forthcoming wedding is made at the time of the engagement of the couple. Such announcements receive much less attention than they did some years ago, and, in fact, there is no longer any absolute need to have the event published in the press at all.

However, there are occasions when an announcement in the advertisement columns of the press is of value to the newly engaged couple – particularly to those who have a very wide circle of friends and acquaintances. In such instances it might well be impractical to write a letter to every one of them.

Sometimes, too, it might be that one or other of the couple (or one of their parents) happens to be a figure of national importance or of wide public interest – a politician or a pop singer perhaps – making the announcement a matter of public interest. Any such announcements, of course, would be enough to bring the reporters and photographers flocking to the door!

In such cases, and where friends and relatives of the couple are widely scattered over the country, the announcements should be made in one or more of the national daily newspapers where a wide circulation is assured. *The Times, The Daily Telegraph, The Guardian* and *The Independent* are four which spring to mind at once as publishing special announcement columns.

If it happens, however, that the friends and relatives are fairly tightly domiciled in a single large city or county, the local newspaper is a better medium in which to advertise than the national morning newspapers and is, of course, considerably less expensive. If the bride and bridegroom do happen to live in districts distant from one another, it might be wise to use the press of each locality in which to announce the engagement and the forthcoming wedding.

The advertisement should be sent to the Classified Advertisements Manager of the newspaper(s) concerned, and should be drafted in the following manner to appear under 'Forthcoming Marriages'.

Mr P J Fry and Miss A Lloyd

The engagement is announced between Peter John Fry, only son of Mr and Mrs G H Fry of Esher, Surrey, and Ann, youngest daughter of Col and Mrs L R Lloyd of Horsham, West Sussex.

It could be varied to read:

The marriage has been arranged and will take place shortly between Peter, only son of Mr and Mrs G H Fry of Esher, Surrey, and Ann, youngest daughter of Col and Mrs L R Lloyd of Horsham, West Sussex.

If, however, the bridegroom has a title or carries a military rank, the wording to the announcement would more probably be as follows:

Flight Lieut P J Fry and Miss A Lloyd

The engagement is announced between Flight Lieutenant Peter John Fry, AFC, RAF, only son of Mr and Mrs G H Fry of Esher, Surrey, and Ann, youngest daughter of Col and Mrs L R Lloyd of Horsham, West Sussex.

Many people use their local newspaper to announce engagements and these normally appear under 'Births, Marriages and Deaths' columns. They tend to be less formal and would read as follows:

LLOYD-FRY – Mr and Mrs Robert Lloyd of Horsham are pleased to announce the engagement of their youngest daughter, Ann, to Peter, only son of Mr and Mrs G H Fry of Esher, Surrey.

And for the groom's local paper:

FRY-LLOYD – Mr and Mrs G H Fry of Esher are pleased to announce the engagement of their only son, Peter, to Ann, youngest daughter of Mr and Mrs Robert Lloyd of Horsham, West Sussex.

If it should be that the bride's father is dead, the second part of the announcement should read:

. . . and Ann, youngest daughter of Mrs Lloyd and the late Col L R Lloyd of Horsham, West Sussex.

If it is the bride's mother who has died, the sentence will read:

. . . and Ann, the youngest daughter of Col L R Lloyd and the late Mrs Lloyd of Horsham, West Sussex.

If the bride's parents have been divorced, the address of each of them should be given, as follows:

. . . and Ann, youngest daughter of Col L R Lloyd of Horsham, West Sussex, and Mrs R L Lloyd of Guildford, Surrey.

If the parents have been divorced and the bride's mother has re-married, the announcement should conclude:

. . . and Ann, youngest daughter of Col L R Lloyd of Horsham, West Sussex, and Mrs C B Brooklyn of Coldharbour, Surrey.

If it is the bridegroom's parents who are either dead or have been divorced, precisely the same amendment should be made to the first part of the announcement as would be made to the second part of the sentence where the bride is concerned.

The day after the wedding a press announcement can appear under the 'Marriages' column. The most usual wording is as follows:

Mr P J Green and Miss A White

The marriage took place on 20th April at the Church of St George, Woodhouse, of Mr Peter J Green, only son of Mr and Mrs A F Green of Esher, Surrey, and Miss Ann White, eldest daughter of Mr and Mrs J F White of Tonbridge, Kent.

Where one party has been divorced the wording could be:

Mr P J Green and Miss A White

A service of blessing was held yesterday at the Church of St Mark, Balham, after the marriage of Mr Peter Green, only son of Mr and Mrs A F Green of Esher, Surrey, and Miss Ann White, eldest daughter of Mr and Mrs F J White of Tonbridge, Kent. The Rev J M Graham officiated.

Or the wording can be simpler:

Mr P J Green and Miss A White

The marriage took place quietly in Baldock on 20th April between Mr Peter J Green and Miss Ann White.

Local papers are often weekly and any marriage announcements sent to such papers should be worded to reflect this.

12

Sending Out The Invitations

In due course invitations to the wedding and the reception need to be printed and despatched by post to those for whom they are intended. The list is a matter for the bride's parents (assuming they are the hosts), as they must select their guests. But it is common and much kinder for the two sets of parents and the engaged couple to consult one another on the subject.

It is reasonable to assume that both the bride and the bridegroom – and their parents – will wish to invite similar numbers from amongst their own relatives and friends, though this is not necessarily the case. For instance, a bridegroom may come from some considerable distance to his wedding; a distance not easily covered by all his friends. Or perhaps the bride is a member of some society which might bring her an unusually large number of friends.

In any event, the bride's parents (as hosts) must be left to make the final decision as to numbers to be invited – at least as far as the reception is concerned; they will be expected to pay the bill for the whole of the entertainment and it could well be an embarrassing amount, although it is becoming more common for both families to share the cost and even for the bride and bridegroom to make a contribution.

Invitations should be sent out well in advance of the event; at least six weeks before the wedding, preferably earlier, so as to give the guests plenty of time to complete their own arrangements and to decline any alternative invitations they may receive to other functions on the same day at the same time. (If anyone among the proposed guest list is a particularly busy person, or the wedding is booked for a busy holiday period, it may be as well to let him or her know the date as soon as it has been fixed in order to avoid the disappointment of some favourite relative or friend being unable to attend.)

The invitations can be printed in a standard fashion, leaving the sender to fill in names in the appropriate places. Any good stationers or printers will have a wide range of wedding stationery available from which a choice can be made. These include invitations (perhaps with a tear off reply slip); Order of Service sheets; menu cards; place cards; serviettes and rings; book matches; ashtrays and drip mats with the bride and groom's Christian names and the wedding date. The stationers may also provide the boxes and cards for sending wedding cake to those unable to attend.

A very popular format for the invitation is:

Colonel and Mrs Leslie R White
request the pleasure of the company of
....
at the marriage of their daughter
Ann
with
Mr Peter John Green
at St George's Parish Church, Ashford
on Saturday, 20th April [date]
at 11 am
and at a reception afterwards at the
Carlton Hotel.

12 Fir Tree Lane
Ashford
Kent   *RSVP*

The RSVP is essential because the hostess must know in advance how many guests she may expect – especially for the meal at the reception.

Of course, the wording of the first part of the invitation will vary with the status of those sending out the invitations. If either of the bride's parents is dead, the name of the surviving parent is sufficient

> *Colonel Leslie R White*
> *requests the pleasure . . .*

or

> *Mrs Joan R White*
> *requests the pleasure . . .*

or the order of the wording could be changed to leave the space for the invitee's name at the top followed by

> *The pleasure of your company*
> *is requested at the marriage of*
> *Ann*
> *daughter of Col Leslie R White and*
> *the late Mrs Joan White . . .*

If the bride's parents are divorced and the wife has re-married or reverted to her maiden name, the invitation should read:

> *Colonel Leslie R White and Mrs Joan Bodkin*
> *request the pleasure . . .*

or, if the wife has not re-married, the following wording may be preferred:

> *Colonel Leslie R White and Joan White*
> *request the pleasure . . .*

Invitations to a register office wedding are similar and would read:

Mr and Mrs A B Cox
request the pleasure of the company of

....

at the marriage of their daughter
Jane
with
Mr James Brown
at the Register Office, Park Road
on Thursday, 10th May [date]
at 11.30 am
and at a reception afterwards at the
Royal Hotel.

12 Dorset Street
Weymouth
Dorset   RSVP

If both parents are dead, the invitations will be issued in the names of the guardians or relatives who are to act as hosts for the occasion, or if the couple are sending the invitations themselves they would, obviously, have their names printed at the top:

Peter Fry and Ann Lloyd
request the pleasure of the company of

....

at their marriage at

Whilst it is usual to combine an invitation to the wedding ceremony and the reception afterwards it is also possible to issue separate invitations. It may be that the couple would prefer a private, family wedding or that the church or register office will only hold a certain number of people. Alternatively, it may be that numbers have to be limited for the wedding breakfast but more people could be invited to an evening reception afterwards. In all variations the wording of the invitation must be completely clear so that the invitees all understand where they are expected and when.

Where the wedding service is a small, family affair and a reception is to be held to include other guests who were not at the ceremony the invitation would read:

Mr and Mrs J S White
request the pleasure of the company of
....
on the evening of the wedding
of their daughter
Maria
with
Mr Peter J Green
at The Park Hotel, Kings Road
at 7.30 pm
on Friday, 7th May [date]

12 Fir Tree Lane
Woodhouse   *RSVP*

An alternative form is:

Mr and Mrs J S White
request the pleasure of the company of
....
at an evening reception
at The Royal Hotel, The Mall
at 7 pm
to celebrate the marriage of their daughter
Susan
with
Mr George Black
on Saturday 30th April [year]

12 Fir Tree Lane
Woodhouse   *RSVP*

It is also possible that if the reception is to take place over the course of an afternoon and evening, with larger numbers attending in the evening, the couple may wish to invite the evening guests to the ceremony itself (especially if it is taking place in a large church). This is quite acceptable and a possible wording for such an invitation is as follows:

Mr and Mrs A B Cox
request the pleasure of the company of
....
at the marriage of their daughter
Jane
with
Mr James Brown
at St Mark's Church, Park Road, Anytown
on Thursday, 10th May [date]
at 11.30 am
and at an evening reception from 7 pm
at the Royal Hotel.

12 Dorset Street
Weymouth
Dorset   *RSVP*

The subject of whether or not to invite children to a wedding is often a fraught one. Many brides do not want their day spoiled by crying or over-excited children and the hosts may object to the additional cost of young guests who neither chose nor wished to attend. Whatever the decision, where a family is being invited it is important to make clear exactly who the invitation applies to. If children are included, their names should be listed; if they are not, the names of the parents only should be listed. Tact and diplomacy may be required but it is the right of the hosts to make the decision and guests should respect that.

If there are to be a number of children at the wedding it could be worth organising a crêche to be run during the service so that the problem of bored children does not occur. This would only be possible where there is a convenient room within or near to the place where the ceremony is taking place and it should be staffed by responsible adults, preferably with plenty of experience in looking after children. Some of the parents may wish to stay with their children, but many will welcome the opportunity to enjoy the wedding without distraction. Don't forget to let guests know that their children should be left at the crêche and send out full instructions as to its location with the invitation.

13

Replies To Invitations

Replies to wedding invitations should be brief and should be despatched without delay. There are many pre-printed reply cards available nowadays which leave a space for the invitee to write their name(s) and if these are not used any written reply should be couched in the third person, such as:

> *15 Winsgrove Terrace*
> *Ellesmere*

Mr and Mrs Joseph Fleet and their daughter, Phyllis, thank Colonel and Mrs Leslie R White for their kind invitation to their daughter's wedding at St George's Parish Church on Saturday 20th April [date] at 11 am and to a reception afterwards at the Carlton Hotel, and are most happy to accept.

11th March [date]

Such a note requires no signature.

It is important that the name of every person planning to attend the wedding is included on the reply. This allows the host to correct any misunderstanding that may have arisen and to ensure that an accurate note of the numbers attending can be kept.

If it is impossible to accept the invitation, either because of a prior engagement or for some private family reason, it is a matter of courtesy both to acknowledge the invitation, and to make the decision not to attend clear. The names of all those unable to attend should be listed.

Again, there are many pre-printed cards available but if the refusal is to be hand written it should be as brief as the acceptance and similarly written in the third person, though an excuse might be added, however vague it may appear to be:

> *15 Winsgrove Terrace*
> *Ellesmere*

> *Mr and Mrs Joseph Fleet and their daughter, Phyllis, thank Colonel and Mrs Leslie R White for their kind invitation to their daughter's wedding at St George's Parish Church on Saturday 20th April [date] and to the reception afterwards.*
>   *Unfortunately they have accepted a prior engagement for that date and must therefore decline with regret.*

> *11th March [date]*

Again, no signature is required.

Sometimes invitations already accepted must later be declined, possibly because of illness, an accident, or even through a sudden death in the family. In such a case the hosts should be informed at once. It may give them time to amend the numbers given to the caterers. A telephone call should be made to the hosts as soon as possible but also a simple note may be appreciated by the hostess, which should make clear who cannot attend if only one of the invited party is affected. Perhaps:

> *15 Winsgrove Terrace*
> *Ellesmere*

> *Mrs Joseph Fleet sincerely regrets the necessity, due to illness, to have to inform you that she will now be unable to attend your daughter's wedding on 20th April [date] or the reception afterwards.*
>   *Mr Joseph Fleet and his daughter, Phyllis, will, however, still be delighted to attend.*

> *14th April [date]*

Again, there is no need for a signature.

Where children are invited the hosts should make this clear on the invitations sent out. If there is any doubt, however, the hosts should be politely asked for clarification. There should be no offence taken if the children are not included – wedding receptions are extremely expensive things to put on and limits have to be set somewhere. Remember that what adults see as a day of celebration and excitement is seen by most children as boring and would test the patience of even the best behaved. If children are invited, parents should be sensitive to the fact that the ceremony itself is a special moment not only for the bride and groom but also for many of the guests. Noisy children will be an unwelcome distraction and sensible parents will agree before the ceremony begins whether one will stay outside with the children or be ready to take them out if they become a nuisance. The same applies when the speeches are being made at the reception.

Presents

There is a certain amount of tradition to be observed in the sending of wedding presents:

(a) Relatives should send a present whether or not they attend the reception and the wedding – so long as they have been invited.

(b) All those attending the wedding ceremony and the reception afterwards are expected to send a present.

(c) There is no need for a friend to send a present when the invitation has been declined – though it is usual to do so when the cause is illness or some other reason that, if it had not arisen, would not have meant a refusal.

(d) There is no need to send a present where the invitation is to the wedding ceremony only – and does not include the reception afterwards.

(e) All presents sent before the wedding should be sent to the bride at her parents' home. If they are sent afterwards, they should be addressed to both the bride and bridegroom at their new home.

(f) If a present is received, it is good manners to invite the giver to the wedding ceremony and usually, though not necessarily, to the reception afterwards. To avoid any embarrassment on this score it is best to wait until invitations to the wedding and the reception have been received before sending presents.

14

Wedding Gifts

Traditionally wedding gifts are sent to the bride at her home (even if the donor is a friend of the groom who has never met the bride). These days, however, many guests take their presents to the reception. The presents may vary from the decorative to the practical, from the purely personal to the 'homey' and from the very expensive to the intrinsically valueless.

Most couples will spend some time compiling a gift list so that when friends telephone to find out what the couple would like as a wedding present they can be given several ideas or even sent a copy of the list. Some couples may feel awkward about doing this but most guests will welcome the opportunity to purchase a gift that the couple really want.

If a list is to be made out it should be specific – giving the product, the manufacturer, the style, colour, etc., and where it can be obtained. A full range of prices should be covered, to give freedom of choice to all the guests. The following outline list is just a guide:

Living Room	*Bedroom*	*Bathroom*
Clock	Pillows	Towels
Cushions	Duvet	Bath mat
Nest of tables	Sheets	Mirror
Lamps	Duvet covers	Linen basket
Music centre	Blankets	Bath rack
Television set	Pillow cases	Indoor clothes line
Video player	Bedspread	Bathroom scales

Vases
Chairs
Settee
Rugs

Bedside clock/
   tea maker
Electric blanket
Long mirror

Towel rail
Soap holder
Shower curtain

Kitchen
Refrigerator/
   freezer
Washing machine
Dishwasher
Cooker
Food mixer
Electric kettle
Coffee percolator
Kitchen knives
Bread board
Toaster
Slow cooker
Microwave oven
Sandwich maker
Mixing bowls
Saucepans
Tea towels
Can opener
Kitchen scales
Pressure cooker
Storage jars
Trays
Wooden spoons
Pedal bin
Washing up bowl
Casserole set
Frying pan
Oven gloves
Spice rack

Dining Room
Dining table
   & chairs
Place mats
Tablecloths
Hostess trolley
Dinner service*
Tea service*
Breakfast set
Salt/pepper mills
Fruit bowl
Cutlery
Water jug
Tumblers
Wine glasses
Sherry glasses
Decanters
Sideboard
Cheese board &
   knife
Hot plate
Candlesticks
Clock

Miscellaneous
Vacuum cleaner
Brushes & mops
Dustpan & brush
Garden furniture
Garden tools
Garden tubs
Shrubs & trees
Lawn mower
Car rug
Picnic set
Ornaments
Wine rack
Wastepaper baskets
Luggage

(*These expensive items could be listed in small lots to make parts that are more generally affordable, i.e. 4 side plates, 4 dinner plates, 4 cups and saucers, etc.)

    Many stores now offer a wedding list service whereby couples can compile their wedding list from the goods the shop sells and register it with the store. People who wish to give a gift can then visit or telephone the store to select and purchase a present, which is then duly deleted from the wedding list. This should ensure that nothing on the list is duplicated. If a national store is chosen it also means that people living all over the country are able to participate easily because while the couple's local branch will hold the list, branches around the country can ring and check what has yet to be bought, or may be able to call up the list on their computer system, and the guests can make their purchase in their own local store. The greatest benefit of this system is that the store takes on the responsibility of managing the wedding present list, a duty which might otherwise have to be undertaken by the bride's mother, sister or chief bridesmaid.

Cheques are often useful to a newly-married couple who will have a hundred and one needs before they complete their home – but, except in the case of fathers, it is not the kind of present that can be suggested with propriety by the bride or her bridegroom. Tokens from local D-I-Y shops can also be useful for couples who will be decorating their new home.

It is important that track is kept of who sent what. An easy way of keeping such a record is for a note to be made on the gift tag accompanying each of the presents as they are unwrapped (but watch that someone doesn't throw them away with the rubbish!). This will be a great help to the couple when they come to write their thank-you letters.

Arrangements could be made for the display of the wedding presents at the reception, and certainly a table should be set aside to store presents brought to the reception by guests. However, the bride and groom will probably not have time to open any gifts on the day of the wedding itself and they may like to show all their presents in their new home or at the bride's mother's home after the wedding or on their return from honeymoon.

Such an exhibition can be made most attractive; tiers of boxes covered by a white table cloth can do much to set off the beauty and interest of the collection of items. Each present should have a card standing beside it on the display tables, giving the donor's name and brief address (such as: John and Sheila Cox, Sheffield). In the case of cheques, only an envelope is displayed stating the name and address of the donor but giving no information concerning its value. Under no circumstances should the cheque itself be displayed. It should be paid into the bank!

A similar restriction should be placed on less usual presents such as an insurance policy, the deeds of a house or share certificates which should be filed safely. Simple cards should represent such items on the display tables, endorsed with the words 'Insurance Policy', 'Deeds of House', or 'Shares Certificate' and the name and brief address of the donor.

Whether a display is made at the reception or not, the bride's parents should remove all the presents to their own home at the end of the celebration. A suitable display could then be arranged for the benefit of friends and neighbours who did not attend the reception. This may well last until a few days before the end of the newly-married couple's honeymoon at which point the gifts should be taken to the couple's home where they, too, may choose to display them once again for the benefit of their own friends.

Security and insurance of the wedding presents must be considered. If gifts are taken to the reception venue for display they should be kept in a locked room until the reception commences, to prevent theft or damage. It may be worth considering extra insurance to cover the gifts while they are at the reception, being transported and even in the home of the bride's parents if they include some very valuable items.

After the honeymoon it is the bride's duty to write and thank the individual donors of presents. Such letters should be sent out as soon as possible after the return from honeymoon but, where the numbers make the task a lengthy one, a verbal message – even over the telephone – will serve as an interim measure. Yet however close the giver and however fulsome the verbal thanks, a letter in due course is a must.

15

A Church Ceremony

We will consider the church ceremony by looking first at the Church of England. However, even if the marriage is to take place in a church which is not Church of England, much of what appears in this chapter will apply, so please read on.

A clergyman of the Church of England may not refuse to perform a marriage service so long as he is sure that there is no legal or ecclesiastical objection to it – and, indeed, he must satisfy himself that the law does in fact specifically permit each particular marriage, since to make a knowingly false declaration is a criminal offence.

Any day of the week may be chosen by the couple as their wedding day, including Sundays and even Good Friday, although the Church does discourage weddings during Lent. It is, of course, necessary for the couple to consult the clergyman concerned to make sure that it is convenient to him and that the church is available.

The most popular days for weddings are Fridays and Saturdays, probably both because it gives the couple an extra weekend for their honeymoon and because it is generally more convenient for their guests. Saturday mornings usually result in a queue of wedding parties at most churches (especially in the summer months) and those who wish to marry at a certain time on a specific day should talk to the clergyman of the church about it well in advance of the projected date – generally months ahead. Preferred times are between 11 am and 4 pm to ensure plenty of time for the reception afterwards.

When the couple have decided on a church they should make an appointment to see the clergyman. Very often he will suggest that they attend a marriage preparation course and, among other things, will discuss what form the service will take.

With the Alternative Service Book 1980, those who wish to be unconventional are given much greater scope by this new service, but it can also be conducted in a very traditional manner. The bridal procession and the ceremony of giving away are optional, and full provision is made for the marriage to take place during a service of Holy Communion.

Two sets of vows are included (with or without the promise to 'obey') which the couple may choose to read instead of repeating after the clergyman. During the vows the bride and groom face each other, and words are provided for the bride either after receiving the ring or on giving a ring to the bridegroom.

The service may incorporate prayers which the couple have written or selected in co-operation with the clergyman and they may choose an appropriate reading or readings from the Bible.

During the scripture reading and sermon the bride and bridegroom may sit in chairs that have been specially placed for them.

The service can be tailored to suit each individual couple so that much of the detail will be decided in consultation with the officiating clergyman.

Many clergymen like to go through the service with each couple in church before the wedding day and have a rehearsal so that everyone is clear who stands where, when to move and generally what to expect. The bridal gown is not needed for this purpose, though it is wise to provide some mock bouquets for young bridesmaids so that they may become accustomed to carrying them when rehearsing their part. Similarly, if a train is to be worn by the bride, a few yards of almost any material will suffice for the rehearsal.

Floral Decorations

The clergyman should also be consulted about the decoration of his church. He has the right to the final say in these arrangements, although he is usually happy for the bride to take full control. White flowers and greenery are usual for weddings but coloured flower arrangements are also very popular, often to match or enhance the bridesmaids' dresses. Lilies, roses, carnations, chrysanthemums and dahlias are often used – with perhaps ferns or evergreens. A vast display is quite unnecessary and any good florist will do the whole thing for you, or perhaps members of the church flower committee may be available to do the arrangements.

Order of Service

A decision has to be made in advance too, concerning the hymns and other music for the service and it is well to consult the organist as soon as possible. Though it is accepted that it is the bride's prerogative to choose the entrance march, hymns, music to be played during the signing of the register and, of course, a wedding march it is obvious that the advice of the clergyman and organist should be taken fully into account. This is particularly applicable where a choir is wanted. (Again, the clergyman has the right to refuse anything which he feels is inappropriate.)

Once all the music has been selected it is possible to arrange the full details of the service on a printed sheet known as the 'Order of Service'. If the bridal couple and the bride's mother complete all these arrangements in good time it is usual to have the Order of Service printed for the use of all who will attend the ceremony. Some couples also like to include details of any readings to be used in the service (book, chapter and verse if from the Bible or title and author if from elsewhere).

Wedding Day Arrangements

On the morning of the wedding the excitement rises. At an early hour the bride will start getting ready, perhaps with her mother's help. An hour or more before the wedding is due to start, the chief bridesmaid should arrive at the bride's home – dressed and ready. She will then help the bride to put the finishing touches to her appearance whilst the bride's mother snatches an opportunity to don her own wedding outfit.

Meanwhile the bridesmaids will begin to congregate at the bride's home; the best man will be arriving at the bridegroom's home, dressed for the ceremony; the ushers will be making ready in their own homes.

Arriving at the church

At least half an hour before the ceremony is due to start, the head usher or groomsman must arrive at the church. Immediately afterwards the other ushers are due and should then receive their final instructions from him.

The head usher will delegate several ushers to direct cars and help them park if necessary. Others will be asked to meet guests at the church door, hand out Order of Service sheets, and conduct the guests to their pews. He will remind them that the bride's mother, brothers and sisters and her grandparents (as appropriate) should be seated in the front pew to the left of the nave facing the altar.

Others of the bride's relatives and friends should be seated on the same side of the church in descending order of relationship and closeness of friendship – so far as is conveniently possible – from the pews immediately behind the bride's mother to the back of the church.

Similarly, the bridegroom's relatives and friends will occupy the pews on the right of the nave. Part of the front row on that side may be needed for the groom and best man before the service and for the best man when the bride and groom go to the altar, so the closer members of his family may have to go in the pews immediately behind.

As a last instruction, the head usher will hand over Order of Service sheets to the other ushers, either to lay in the pews in advance, or, more usually, to hand out as they conduct the wedding party and the guests to their seats.

Meanwhile, the best man should be making quite certain that the bridegroom is properly dressed for his wedding. He should also check the items he must take with him – the wedding ring (or rings) in his waistcoat pocket, money in his hip pocket to pay the marriage fees if they have not been paid at the time of a rehearsal, and the couple's rail, boat or air tickets, passports and hotel reservations in his inside pocket.

He should conduct the bridegroom to the church in order to arrive at least 20 minutes before the service is due to start. They then usually find themselves some secluded spot in which to wait. The clergyman often takes this opportunity to check details for the register.

From about now on, the guests begin to arrive and must be conducted to their seats. (Though in the past it was usual for women always to wear some form of head-dress in church, there is now no obligation on them to do so. However, many women – in particular, the mothers of the bride and groom – will wish to wear a hat as part of their wedding outfit.) Those who have not met for some time, and those who are meeting for the first time, will be inclined to chat at the church door, causing a little obstruction and possibly creating a hold-up when the bride arrives. A gentle hint here and there should get them to their places in ample time, however.

The chief bridesmaid should arrive in company with the other bridesmaids and pages, not less than five minutes before the bride is due. They should gather in the church porch ready to form a procession and, again, though the guests will tend to stop and talk to them, they should be dissuaded as much as possible as time will be getting short.

At the time the bridesmaids arrive, the best man should lead the bridegroom along the nave to the chancel steps – the best man on the bridegroom's right – though often the groom and best man wait in the front pew until the first notes of the wedding march.

The arrival, entrance and procession of the bridal party is one of the high spots of pageantry for the occasion and it is important, therefore, that everybody should be in their places in good time. The bride and her father arrive at the church last but they should be exactly on time. In areas where traffic is busy it is well for them to leave home early, even if it means that they have to cruise around for a few minutes to adjust their arrival to the exactly scheduled time. Great panic can be caused by the bride who arrives early!

Nor must this be an occasion when the bride exercises a woman's right to be late. It would be discourteous to the clergyman, the organist and the guests – not to mention the nervous groom – and besides, it may cause serious delay to someone else's wedding which may be due to take place immediately afterwards.

A few photographs may be taken as the bride walks towards the church on her father's arm. The chief bridesmaid should make any last minute adjustments to the bride's dress.

The organist will be alerted to the bride's arrival and move over from the introductory music to the wedding march. With his daughter on his right arm, her father will lead her forward into the body of the church, in slow time – the pages and the bridesmaids taking up their places in the procession, in pairs, with the chief bridesmaid just behind the bride and her father.

The officiating clergyman (and sometimes the choir) may meet

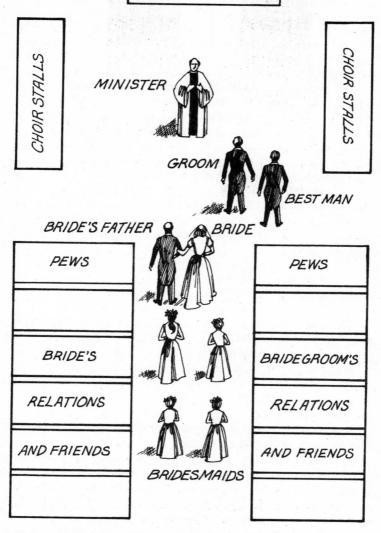

ALTAR

CHOIR STALLS

CHOIR STALLS

MINISTER

GROOM

BEST MAN

BRIDE'S FATHER   BRIDE

PEWS

PEWS

BRIDE'S

BRIDEGROOM'S

RELATIONS

RELATIONS

AND FRIENDS

AND FRIENDS

BRIDESMAIDS

1. The procession.

the bride at the door and precede her down the aisle or he may await the bride on the chancel steps. During the processional the bride's attention must not wander. Her gaze should be directed towards the clergyman or the altar, until she stands beside her bridegroom. To effect a properly paced procession, the bride and her father should move off with the left foot in time with the march, those following picking up the step as they fall in behind.

The bridegroom and his best man should turn to welcome the bride as she approaches and her father should lead her to the bridegroom's left. As they face the altar and the clergyman, they stand, from left to right: the bride's father, the bride, the bridegroom and the best man.

Once they are in position, with the bridesmaids standing in pairs behind the bride, the chief bridesmaid should step forward (just as her father releases the bride's arm) to take the bouquet and set the bride's veil clear of her face, back over her head. The chief bridesmaid then returns to her place immediately behind the bride, satisfying herself that the bridesmaids and pages are in their places too.

The service and ceremony

At the beginning of the service, once the bridal party is in place in front of the clergyman, a hymn is often sung. This gives the couple an opportunity to relax a little. The clergyman then begins the chosen service, stating the reason for the gathering in the church, the reason for matrimony, followed by a demand to know if there is any impediment to the marriage, first from the congregation, and then from the couple. To guard against malicious allegations the clergyman may demand a bond from anyone alleging impediment.

If he is satisfied that there is no legal objection to the union, he will then ask the man:

'Wilt thou have this woman to thy wedded wife, to live together according to God's law in the holy estate of matrimony? Wilt thou love her, comfort her, honour and keep her, in sickness and in health? And, forsaking all other, keep thee only unto her, so long as ye both shall live?'

The man shall answer: 'I will.'

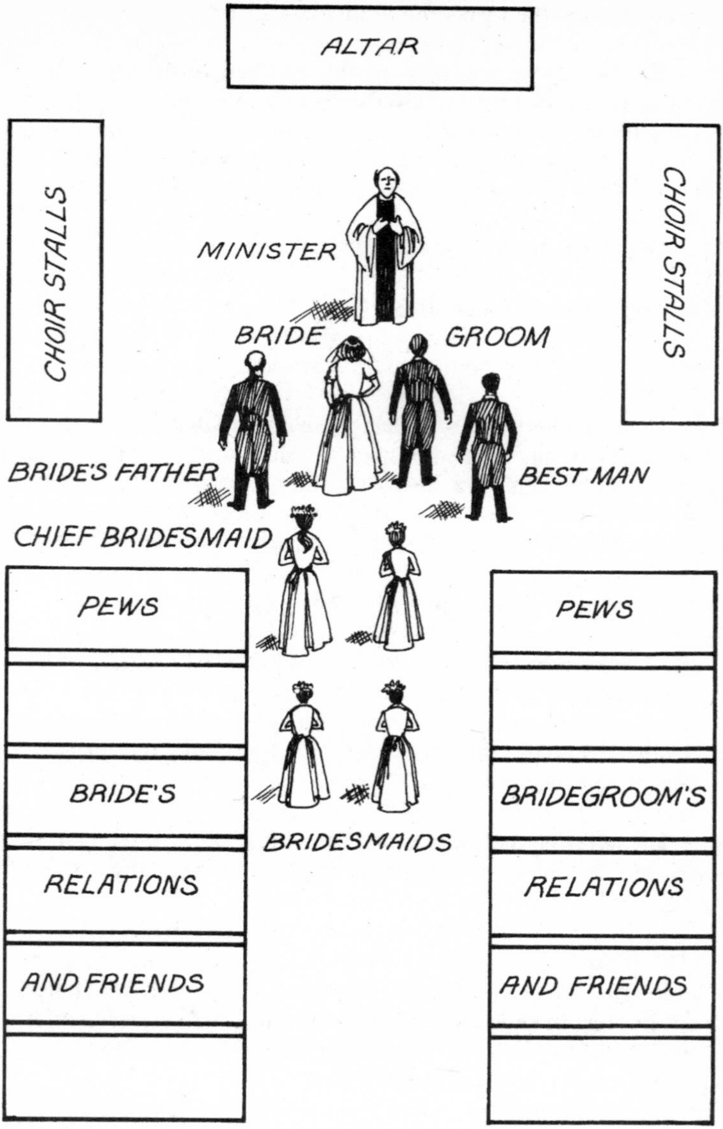

ALTAR

CHOIR STALLS

CHOIR STALLS

MINISTER

BRIDE   GROOM

BRIDE'S FATHER   BEST MAN

CHIEF BRIDESMAID

PEWS   PEWS

BRIDE'S   BRIDEGROOM'S

BRIDESMAIDS

RELATIONS   RELATIONS

AND FRIENDS   AND FRIENDS

2. Positions during the service.

The clergyman then asks the woman:

> 'Wilt thou have this man to thy wedded husband, to live together according to God's law in the holy estate of matrimony? Wilt thou love him, comfort him, honour and keep him, in sickness and in health? And, forsaking all other, keep thee only to him, so long as ye both shall live?'

The woman shall answer: 'I will.'

The clergyman will then ask:

> 'Who giveth this woman to be married to this man?'

Immediately, the bride's father passes his daughter's right hand to the clergyman, palm downwards. He passes it into the hand of the bridegroom. The bride's father's part in the service is now ended and he may, if he wishes, drop back and take his place in the front pew beside his wife, as unobtrusively as possible.

The bridegroom will then say after the clergyman:

> 'I ... take thee ... to my wedded wife, to have and to hold from this day forward, for better, for worse: for richer for poorer; in sickness and in health; to love and to cherish, till death us do part, according to God's holy law; and thereto I give thee my troth.'

The pair will free their hands and then the bride will take the right hand of the man in her own right hand and say after the clergyman:

> 'I ... take thee ... to my wedded husband, to have and to hold from this day forward, for better, for worse: for richer, for poorer; in sickness and in health; to love and to cherish, till death us do part, according to God's holy law; and thereto I give thee my troth.'

As they free their hands, the best man takes the wedding ring from his waistcoat pocket and places it on the surface of the open prayer book proffered by the clergyman. After a prayer for the blessing of the ring, the clergyman will offer it to the bridegroom who will take it and place it on the third finger of his bride's left hand. (She should have transferred her engagement ring to her right hand before leaving for the church.)

While the bridegroom holds the ring in place, he must repeat after the clergyman:

'With this ring I thee wed; with my body I thee honour; and all my worldly goods with thee I share: In the Name of the Father, and of the Son, and of the Holy Ghost. Amen.'

It is often the case these days that the bride wishes to give a ring to the bridegroom. When this is so, the best man gives both rings to the clergyman and they are both blessed. The bride puts the ring on the bridegroom's finger after she herself has received the ring he is giving her, either silently or both say the words together.

The above wording is according to the Alternative Services, First Series. Sometimes a couple chooses to be married with the words of the 1662 Prayer Book, which includes the promise by the bride to obey her husband.

(Couples also have the choice of using the wedding service from the Alternative Service Book 1980 in which the introduction and various elements of the service are different. The clergyman may give a short address. A hymn may be sung instead of the psalm. The Alternative Service Book provides for prayers written or chosen by the couple in consultation with the clergyman.)

This concludes the official ceremony and is followed by the nuptial blessing, prayers and a psalm.

As soon as it is over the clergyman or verger will lead the way to the vestry, or sometimes a chapel, followed in procession by the newly-married couple, the bridegroom's father with the bride's mother, the bride's father with the bridegroom's mother, the best man and the chief bridesmaid, the other bridesmaids and pages and perhaps one or two others.

In the vestry the bride signs the register – in her maiden name probably for the last time (though legally she may choose whether or not to take her husband's surname in the future) – followed by her husband, the clergyman and two witnesses, often the best man and the chief bridesmaid. The choice of witnesses should be made well in advance and is limited by the fact that a witness must be over 18 years of age. Everyone should be made aware of who the witnesses are, to prevent any confusion arising when the bridal party go to sign the register.

As soon as the registration is completed, the organist will get the signal and immediately the bridal couple will start the recessional. The bride will walk with her hand on her husband's left arm and with her veil thrown clear of her face. The chief bridesmaid and best man will follow behind the newly-weds, with the rest of the bridesmaids behind them. They are followed by the bride's father with the groom's mother and the bride's mother with the groom's father.

During the recessional there is no reason why the bridal couple should not smile and nod to their friends as they walk slowly down the nave but there must be no pause or conversation inside the church. (The best man may slip out to reach the church door in advance of the bridal party, if the church has a suitable exit, but if this is to happen the chief bridesmaid should be warned in advance so that she isn't confused by his absence.)

It is usually possible to have the church bells pealed for up to half an hour after the ceremony where a church possesses them (and for twenty minutes immediately prior to the ceremony, if so desired). There will, of course, be an extra charge for this and the organist should be consulted, together with the verger.

After the service
There is likely to be considerable delay at this point. As well as the official photographer, a number of friends of the bride and groom will want to take the opportunity to photograph the newly-weds, their bridesmaids, the official party – and, indeed, the church and the rest of the congregation, as it strolls out into the light of day.

As a sort of Master of Ceremonies, the best man needs to keep a check on the time. The whole party is due to arrive at the reception rooms at a pre-stated time and if there is any unnecessary delay, the result might be a cold meal or a very short reception.

Just before the bridal couple get into their car for the journey to the reception, confetti or rice is normally thrown over them. However, if the clergyman requested at the beginning of the

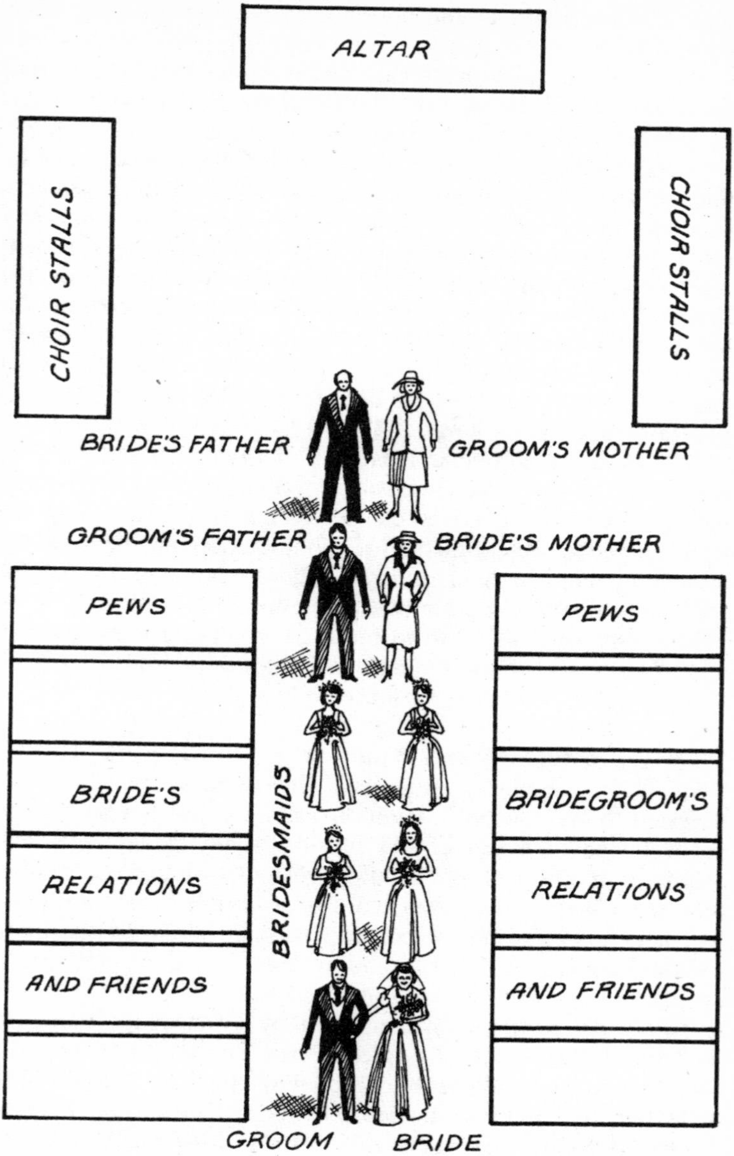

ALTAR

CHOIR STALLS

CHOIR STALLS

BRIDE'S FATHER

GROOM'S MOTHER

GROOM'S FATHER

BRIDE'S MOTHER

PEWS

PEWS

BRIDE'S

BRIDEGROOM'S

RELATIONS

RELATIONS

AND FRIENDS

AND FRIENDS

BRIDESMAIDS

GROOM

BRIDE

3. The recessional.

service that confetti should not be used because it causes litter, the guests should, of course, refrain from using it.

The best man must make sure that the bride and her husband leave for the reception first, followed in succession by their parents, bridesmaids, family and guests.

He may have one last duty to perform at the church before he himself follows: he may still have to settle the bridegroom's expenses in the form of marriage fees, organist's fees and any other out-of-pocket expenses that may have arisen on the spot. All fees are usually settled well before the day, but, if not, the best man has this duty at the service. If there is no opportunity for him to have a word with the clergyman before or afterwards, there is no objection to the fees being placed in a sealed envelope and given to the verger to be delivered in due course. Fees are generally paid in one lump.

(If, for some particular reason, a clergyman other than the incumbent of the church where the wedding ceremony is to be held is invited to conduct the service, it is usual to pay the marriage fee to each of them. Such an invitation may be extended to a clergyman who happens to be a close relative or a particular friend of either the bride or the bridegroom.)

The best man will need to be at the reception fairly quickly and, if he is wise, he will either have one of the ushers standing by with a car, or arrange for a taxi to be available.

Marriage of Widows and Widowers

Though the ceremony is exactly the same where the bride happens to be a *widow*, tradition calls for less formality and suggests the omission of the full bridal gown, and the veil. Similarly, the bridegroom should wear a dark lounge suit rather than the formal attire often worn at a bride's 'first' wedding. Not later than the day before her 'second' wedding, the bride should remove her 'first' wedding ring – and never wear it again.

The bride is often not supported by bridesmaids though a matron of honour usually attends her, chosen from amongst sisters (her own or the bridegroom's) or close friends. The bridegroom should be attended by a best man. Ushers may be brought in, but as the ceremony is usually less ostentatious and less formal, there is rarely any need for them at a bride's 'second' marriage.

If there is no procession before the service, the matron of honour should wait for the bride at the chancel steps and her only duty is to relieve the bride of her bouquet. Nor is there any obligation on anyone to 'give the bride away', though she may invite her father or some other male relative to do so.

The ceremony tends to be simple but the same restriction need not be placed on the reception afterwards – if there has been some lapse of time since the bride's first husband died. In such a case a wedding cake, floral decorations and speeches are quite permissible. If the wedding takes place within a year of the first husband's death, however, some people might find it more appropriate for the service and the reception afterwards to be confined to members of the bride and bridegroom's family and only a very few friends.

The marriage of a *widower* is much less restricted by convention than in the case of a widow. However, it is still commonly less formal than a first wedding – but the decision is that of the bride. Her wishes should be followed in the matter of the service, the formality, the number of guests and the scale of the reception afterwards.

The bride would be quite in order if she wore a formal bridal gown and a veil, was attended by bridesmaids and was 'given away' by her father.

Divorcees

Though the civil law permits the re-marriage of divorced persons, it is forbidden by the law of the Church of England. Nor can a clergyman be compelled to permit the re-marriage of a divorced person by anyone else in his church.

This means that no marriage service can be performed in a church of the Church of England where either the bride or the bridegroom have a previous partner still living, unless the clergyman is prepared to ignore the church authorities and follow the civil law.

However, ecclesiastical authority does allow for a service of prayer and dedication (often called a 'Blessing Service') which may follow a civil wedding. This must not pretend to be a wedding and there are no legal formalities. This service of blessing can be held in a church, or before the reception at the bride's home, in a marquee, hotel or hired hall, if the clergyman is willing to officiate.

Double Wedding

That is, the marriage of two couples before the same clergyman (or Superintendent Registrar of Marriages) at the same time and in the same ceremony. This is by no means a rare occurrence.

Less common are ceremonies binding three separate couples in wedlock at the same time.

Larger groups are not unknown and, indeed, there is nothing to prohibit a mass wedding, linking together any number of couples at the same time. However, the cause for such massive ceremonies is rare in this country and multiple weddings are more often than not confined to family celebrations. Most common of all such occasions is the simultaneous marriage of sisters, or of twins, to their chosen partners.

A double wedding calls for precisely the same detailed prior arrangements as those applicable to anybody about to marry. Each one of them must give the same notice; each couple must be separately licenced and, of course, distinct certificates of marriage will be issued to each of the couples.

The brides will have their own bridesmaids and a best man will be chosen by each of the bridegrooms. The brides will walk down the aisle side-by-side to join their waiting bridegrooms. The two couples will then stand before the clergyman side-by-side, each bridegroom on the right of his bride.

The single ceremony will embrace both couples and only the responses will be made individually.

The recession must generally be made in separate parties because of the narrowness of the usual aisle, each party being complete in itself. The leading couple will assume that place by arrangement and not because of any 'right', though it is usual to allow the elder of the two men to escort his bride and their attendants from the church first.

Video Recordings of the Ceremony

Many couples like to have a video tape taken of their wedding day, including the ceremony and often the reception afterwards. This could be done by the official photographer or some other person but the clergyman and the organist should be consulted about this in advance of the wedding day in case there are any restrictions. The clergyman has the legal right to have the final say, although most are happy for this to take place provided the video camera operator will be discreet and unobtrusive. There may also be copyright implications regarding the hymns and any other music played during the service (the organist will be able to give advice on such matters). Also, the Parochial Church Council will normally charge a fee for the use of a video camera in church (the clergyman will be able to give exact details).

16

The Ceremony By Other Rites, And Civil Marriages

The Roman Catholic Church

There are two types of service for those marrying within the rites of the Roman Catholic church: the 'Marriage celebrated during Mass' and the 'Marriage celebrated outside Mass'.

In each ceremony the first part is identical. This consists of the Entrance Rite, the Liturgy of the Word, and the Rite of Marriage. Where the Mass is to be celebrated, the Liturgy of the Eucharist follows during which it is customary for the Catholics who are present to receive Holy Communion.

In the Roman Catholic Church a 'mixed marriage' is one between a Roman Catholic and someone who has been baptised in another Christian church, and a marriage between a Roman Catholic and someone who has not been baptised.

A marriage celebrated during Mass is usually considered appropriate in a marriage between Roman Catholics. A couple in a mixed marriage may discuss this with the priest.

A marriage between a Catholic and a baptised non-Catholic requires express permission from the Catholic party's parish priest. A marriage between a Catholic and a non-baptised person needs a dispensation, obtainable through the parish priest.

In either case the Catholic party has to undertake to avoid the danger of falling away from the faith, and sincerely to promise to do everything possible 'within the unity of the partnership' to ensure the Catholic baptism and upbringing of all children of the marriage. Also, the priest must be able to sign a statement saying that, in his opinion, the non-Catholic will not oppose the fulfilment of the promise made by the Catholic. Such a marriage will normally take place in the Catholic church; for good reasons, a dispensation *can* be granted for it to be celebrated in the church of the other Christian partner.

In any event it is essential for the couple to consult the clergyman who is to conduct the service at least six months in advance. This gives plenty of time for the ironing out of any 'snags' that may exist, ensures that the date and time of the ceremony can be fixed without clashing with any other arrangements and allows the clergyman to prepare both parties before marrying them in his church. Indeed, it is increasingly common for all couples who are marrying in the Catholic Church to be asked to attend some form of 'preparation'. This is wider than 'religious instruction', and covers a number of points which are common to *all* marriages. The purpose of this is to try to ensure that the couple are prepared adequately for marriage and have a reasonable understanding of what they are doing.

It is customary in both forms of the Catholic marriage service for the bride to be accompanied into the church either by one of her parents or a near relative. The bride is accompanied to the bridegroom standing before the altar, with the best man on his right. It is also possible for the bride and bridegroom to enter the church together, and be greeted at the entrance by the priest and members of the family. The couple may then lead family and friends into the church. The current Rite of Marriage allows for both forms of entry. The Rite also allows for both the traditional gesture in which the bride is 'given away' by her father (or whoever accompanied her into the church) or, alternatively, for the bride simply to offer her hand to the bridegroom. The chief bridesmaid stations herself slightly behind the bride, on her left, after attending to the wedding veil and taking charge of the bridal bouquet. The bridesmaids stand in a line behind, facing the altar.

After the exchange of vows there follows the blessing of the ring(s). The husband places the ring on his wife's finger with the words: '. . . (Christian name only), take this ring as a sign of my love and fidelity. In the name of the Father, and of the Son, and of the Holy Spirit.' If there are two rings, the wife places a ring on her husband's finger saying the same words. At the end of the ceremony the bridal couple sign the register accompanied by at least two witnesses.

The bride and bridegrooms will need to choose music, hymns and readings to be used in the service, in consultation with the priest (and the organist). They will be invited to read out the passages from the scripture themselves during the ceremony or to invite relatives or friends to do so. The priest or deacon will read the Gospel passage. This is where the couple can bring their own personal 'touch' to the proceedings, by choosing a piece from the scripture, hymns and music which have, perhaps, special meaning for them. Naturally, if the scripture passage and music chosen are pertinent to the wedding service, so much the better, and this can make the whole proceedings fuller and richer. The selected readings can be included on the Order of Service sheets if they have been selected far enough in advance (book, chapter and verse if from the Bible or title and author if from elsewhere).

On signing the register the bride will use her maiden name, probably for the last time (although, legally, she does not have to take the name of her husband upon marriage). The witnesses who are to sign the register should be chosen well in advance; this prevents any confusion arising when the chosen group proceed to the Sanctuary. The usual persons chosen to accompany the bridal pair as witnesses of the signatures are the best man and the chief bridesmaid, but in any event, each person who is to act as a witness should be 18 years of age or over. Bear this in mind if you have chosen a particularly young chief bridesmaid or best man.

When the ceremony is concluded, the protocol afterward, when the bride and bridegroom leave the Sanctuary, is for the bridesmaids and best man to take up places behind the bridal couple – the chief bridesmaid on the right arm of the best man, other bridesmaids and pageboys following in pairs. The procession then moves in the recessional down the aisle to the church door. Now is the time for the photographers to move in and snap the group, including the wedding guests who have now left the church door.

Afterwards, the whole party proceeds to the scene of the wedding reception.

The re-marriage of divorced persons is strictly refused in the Catholic Church. However, there may be cases where a previous marriage is not recognised by the Church: when a declaration of nullity of the previous marriage has been granted by the Catholic Church, or if a previous marriage has not complied with Church Law. In these cases, a church marriage would normally be permitted.

The Free Churches

In the majority of Free Church denominations the church itself will have been registered by a Superintendent Registrar of Marriages as a building in which marriages may be solemnised. Ministers of the United Reformed Church, the Baptist, Methodist and other Protestant churches have long taken advantage of their rights, under the Marriage Act of 1898, to become registered as 'authorised' persons; that is, to have applied for and received sanction both to conduct the service and to act as the registrar under the civil law.

Others, for various reasons, have not sought such authority and, in consequence, though they may conduct a marriage ceremony, a superintendent registrar or his deputy must be present to record the wedding, or a separate civil ceremony must be conducted by a superintendent registrar in his office.

Whether or not the minister conducting the service is an authorised person, proper notice of the intention to marry must be given in accordance with civil law and the service must take place in a registered building. Also, wherever the venue of a marriage, the register must be signed by the bridal couple after they have made their vows and the fact must be acknowledged by the signatures of two witnesses.

The minister concerned should be consulted well in advance of the projected date of the wedding so that the church can be booked and in order to ensure plenty of time for all the other necessary arrangements to be made. In all cases, the order of service is a matter left almost entirely to the religious scruples of the couple who are to be married, and, of course, to the special rites of the church whose blessing they seek. At some point in the service, however, declarations must be made in the presence of the minister (or some authorised member of the church) or before a registrar in the couple's choice of the following prescribed words:

i) Declaratory words

'I do solemnly declare that I know not of any lawful impediment why I ... may not be joined in matrimony to ...'

or

'I declare that I know of no legal reason why I ... may not be joined in marriage to ...'

or

by replying 'I am' to the question: 'Are you . . . free lawfully to marry . . .?'

ii) Contracting words (to each other in turn)
'I call upon these persons here present to witness that I . . . do take thee . . . to my lawful wedded husband (or wife).'
or
'I . . . take you . . . to be my wedded wife (or husband).'
or
'I . . . take thee . . . to be my wedded wife (or husband).'

The differences between the ceremonies of the different denominations are considerable – sometimes merely a matter of detail, sometimes they are fundamental. Some churches are more ornate in their ceremonial than others, some more formal and yet others are extremely simple. In almost every case, however, the order of service roughly follows that customary in the Church of England, some details of which include:

1. The procession during which the bride enters and comes to stand before the minister, to the left of her bridegroom, her father (or whoever is to give her away) on her left. The best man stands on the right of the bridegroom.
2. The service usually begins with a prayer and a hymn, followed by a declaration of the purpose of marriage.
3. The minister will call upon the congregation to voice any legal objection to the marriage.
4. The couple exchange vows as required by law and then give and receive a ring or rings.
5. The couple receive the blessing of the church.
6. The register is signed by the couple and two witnesses.
7. The bridal party leave the church to the recessional.

The minister (and organist) should be consulted before any Order of Service sheet is printed, regarding the selection of hymns, music and readings and the order in which things will take place throughout the service.

Although it is general for the Free Churches to view a marriage as binding for life, it is usually within the discretion of each minister to consider the re-marriage of a divorced person, examining each individual case in the light of its own merits.

Some ministers may be adamant in their refusal to marry a person who has been divorced, others will take note of who was the injured party and yet others may consider the whole circumstances surrounding the breakdown of a former marriage. Where one of the couple is divorced, therefore, careful enquiries need to be made before any arrangements are completed.

It should be remembered that although the clergyman of a Parish Church *must* conduct the marriage of any couple legally free to marry (both parties marrying for the first time), a Free Church minister does not have to. He may impose a faith requirement and may refuse to conduct the marriage service for reason of lack of faith on the part of the engaged couple.

The Quakers (Religious Society of Friends)

A Quaker marriage is very different from most other wedding services. It is extremely simple and altogether free of ceremonial.

The first step to such a marriage needs to be taken at least six weeks in advance of the proposed date when application should be made to the registering officer of the monthly meeting within the bounds of which it is proposed that the marriage should take place. For each non-Quaker applicant, support in writing must be obtained from two adult members of the Society, given on forms which the registering officer will supply; if the registering officer assents to the application he will supply the party or parties with the appropriate form for the superintendent registrar.

The couple must then make application to marry in accordance with civil law through the Superintendent Registrar of Marriages in the district in which they live – or if they live in different districts, notice must be given to the registrar in each district.

Notice of the intended marriage is given by the Quaker registering officer at the Sunday morning meeting or meetings to which the parties belong or which they usually attend or in the area in which they live. If no written objection is received, the registering officer will ask the appropriate meeting to appoint a meeting for worship for the solemnisation of the marriage. Public notice of such a meeting will be given at the place at which it is to be held, at the close of the previous meeting for worship.

The service, as any Quaker meeting, is held on the basis of silent communication of the spirit: there is neither pageantry nor music, set service nor sermon; there is, however, opportunity for those who may feel moved by the spirit to give a spoken message of prayer. There is not necessarily a bridesmaid or a best man; a morning coat is unusual and the bride's dress will be fairly simple; there is neither a procession nor a recessional afterwards. But at some point during the meeting the bride and groom will rise and, hand-in-hand, make their declaration of marriage.

The bridegroom will say:

'Friends, I take this my friend . . . to be my wife, promising, through divine assistance, to be unto her a loving and faithful husband, so long as we both on earth shall live.'

The bride makes a similar declaration. The wedding certificate is then signed by the bridal couple and by two of the witnesses. The certificate is read aloud by the registering officer and after the meeting it is usual for all others present to add their names to it. The wedding ring plays no official part in the marriage, though it is common for the couple either to exchange rings afterwards or for the groom to give one to his bride.

It is usual at the close of the meeting for worship for the couple to withdraw with four witnesses and the registering officer to complete the civil marriage register.

The Society retains its belief in the sanctity and life-long nature of marriage, but recognises that in certain circumstances it may be right to make a new start, and the re-marriage of a divorced person may be allowed at the discretion of the monthly meeting.

The Jewish wedding

Synagogue marriage in Britain is both a civil and religious ceremony. The requirements of both must be satisfied before the marriage can take place. Two separate applications for permission to marry are necessary.

Each party makes a personal visit, about twelve weeks before the wedding, to the register office of their home district. After 21 days the superintendent registrar issues his Certificate of Marriage. This must be sent or brought to the office authorising the synagogue marriage. Marriage at short notice can be arranged by a special licence obtainable from the registrar for an additional fee.

Those wishing to marry under the auspices of the Chief Rabbi must attend the Marriage Authorisation Office (see Appendix for address) or the religious authority under which their ceremony is to take place. This meeting should occur 3–4 months prior to the proposed wedding date. Outside London, the local Minister or Secretary for Marriages can arrange this.

Normally on the Sabbath prior to the wedding, the bridegroom is called up to the Reading of the Law in Synagogue.

It is customary for bride and groom to fast on the wedding day until after the ceremony, although there are some days in the Jewish calendar which are exceptions to this rule.

Etiquette at the Synagogue can vary. However, the groom is always expected to arrive first. He sits in a place of honour, sometimes the seats allocated to the Wardens of the Synagogue, with his father, future father-in-law and best man.

The groom takes his place first under the *chuppah* (wedding canopy), the best man stands behind and to his left, ready to hand over the ring.

The bride can be brought in either by her father and mother, or by her mother and the groom's mother, followed by bridesmaids and other relatives. There is no hard and fast rule. The *Unterfuhrers*, as those who accompany the bride and groom are called, also stand beneath the *chuppah*.

Before the bride comes under the *chuppah* the groom is formally requested by the Minister to approve the appointment of two witnesses who sign the *ketubah* (marriage document) and accept the terms and conditions of the *ketubah* whereby he undertakes a number of obligations to his wife. The bride stands under the *chuppah* at the groom's right.

The ceremony begins with a chant of welcome, followed by the blessings of betrothal which are recited over a cup of wine. The first blessing is for the wine itself and the second praises God for the commandment to marry and the implicit restrictions which concern any forbidden marriages. If the Minister wishes to give spiritual guidance and personal blessing to the couple, he will do this before the commencement of the blessings of betrothal.

In Jewish law, the couple become married when the man places the ring on the woman's finger and makes the declaration 'Behold thou art consecrated unto me by this ring according to the Law of Moses and of Israel.' The woman's consent is signified by her acceptance of the ring. It is important to note that this act effecting their union is carried out by the parties themselves; it is not the Minister who 'marries' them, but they who marry each other, and the Minister's presence is as a Jewish law expert, and sometimes as witness to the *ketubah* as well as in a civil capacity if he is Secretary for Marriages.

Since the ring has such importance, it must be the groom's property, should be circular in make and in precious metal (but without jewels), and the bride should wear no other rings or jewellery during the ceremony. The ring is placed on the bride's right index finger, but she may transfer it to the 'ring finger' later. The reason for Jewish insistence on a plain ring is to allow no difference between rich and poor and to avoid any deception or misunderstanding as to its value. It is placed on the right index finger because in ancient transactions this finger was used symbolically to acquire things.

The *ketubah* is now read out loud in Aramaic original. An English abstract follows. The bride should look after the *ketubah* carefully since it is her interests which it recognises, and should it be lost she should get it replaced.

Then follow the Seven Blessings of Marriage, recited over a cup of wine. These words of prayer call upon the Almighty to help the bride and groom find the perfect happiness of Adam and Eve and live a life of 'joy and gladness, mirth and exultation, pleasure and delight, love and brotherhood, peace and companionship'. The couple then sip wine from separate cups given to them by their respective mothers-in-law. This is followed by the breaking of a glass by the groom – a custom that dates back to Talmudic times.

The ceremony concludes by the Minister pronouncing the blessing of the Priests found in the Bible, in the heartfelt wish that its words of blessing, protection, grace and peace be fulfilled for bride and groom.

The couple sign the civil marriage documents, the bride signing her maiden name. The group leave the Synagogue in procession with their attendants. Before greeting their guests at the reception they will spend a short period of time together in private (*yihud*) denoting their newly-acquired status as husband and wife, entitled to live together under the same roof. Having (in most cases) been fasting since dawn on the day of their wedding, they will now break their fast and have their first meal together as husband and wife.

Civil marriages

Nowadays, more and more people are choosing to marry through a civil ceremony. There are many reasons for this – perhaps because the couple have no religious beliefs, or perhaps one or both of the parties is divorced, or perhaps for other reasons.

Before the issue of a Superintendent Registrar's Certificate, 21 days must elapse following the giving of notice. Where the couple apply for a Superintendent Registrar's Licence and satisfy the requirements for the issue of such a document the ceremony may be performed by the superintendent registrar after the expiration of one clear working day, except a Sunday, Good Friday or Christmas Day, from the date of the entry of the notice. (See Chapter 3 for the legal requirements with regard to the issue of a Superintendent Registrar's Certificate or Licence.)

Such a marriage entails no religious service; all that is expected is that the couple's choice of the following vows be exchanged before a superintendent registrar and two witnesses:

'I do solemnly declare that I know not of any lawful impediment why I, . . ., may not be joined in matrimony to . . .'

or

'I declare that I know of no legal reason why I, . . ., may not be joined in marriage to . . .'

or

by replying 'I am' to the question 'Are you . . . free lawfully to marry . . .?'

The couple must also say to each other one of the following statements:

'I call upon these persons here present to witness that I, . . ., do take thee, . . ., to be my lawful wedded wife (or husband)'.

or

'I . . . take you . . . to be my wedded wife (or husband).'

or

'I . . . take thee . . . to be my wedded wife (or husband).'

Then follows the signing of the marriage register by each of the newly-weds and those witnessing the event.

The symbol of the wedding ring(s), given by the bridegroom to the bride or exchanged between the couple, is common practice but has no legal significance under civil law.

A register office wedding can be as informal or as dressy as the parties concerned wish to make it. It can be a very simple and small affair, with informal dress, and perhaps just the two necessary witnesses accompanying the bride and groom. On the other hand, it may be conducted in full bridal regalia (the bride in a long white dress, attended by bridesmaids and pages, and the groom, best man and male guests in morning dress); as many guests as can be accommodated in the wedding room can attend the ceremony; there can be flower arrangements to complement the bridal party; everything can be done to make the ceremony as 'special' as possible. (It has been known for brides to arrive at some register offices in horse drawn carriages or white Rolls Royces.)

However, a register office wedding is restricted in many ways – size of room, lack of time, uninspiring surroundings – and many people prefer to take advantage of the 1994 Marriage Act (England and Wales) which allows a civil wedding to take place in any approved premises (see page 29). This means that the wedding ceremony can be personalised and extended to a much greater degree than is possible in a busy register office. Again, no religious element is allowed because it is a civil ceremony but the couple may add secular readings and music and generally make it special in their own way, provided due regard is given to the solemn nature of the event. In many instances the ceremony and reception both take place in the same building, although that is not necessarily the case.

The superintendent registrar should be consulted if a civil wedding is planned – either in a register office or in some other approved premises. (A book listing all the approved premises in England and Wales is available for purchase from the office of the Registrar General in Southport, but a list of venues in each registration district is available from the local register office.) Possible dates should be discussed with the registrar as well as the chosen venue for both the wedding and the reception in advance of any firm bookings being made because a registrar will need to be available to conduct the ceremony (and two will have to attend a civil ceremony which is not held in a register office).

The civil law takes no notice of religious beliefs or scruples in the case of the re-marriage of divorcees. So long as the decree absolute has been granted and all other legal requirements have been met, the superintendent registrar is duty bound to perform such a marriage ceremony.

17

Celebrations

After the wedding ceremony comes the reception and this can be as formal or informal as the couple wish to make it. The main criteria will be how much money is to be spent and how many guests have to be invited. This will help make the decision as to whether the reception is to be held in the bride's home, quite often with a marquee in the garden to give added space, in a village or church hall where there are usually tables, chairs, cloakrooms and kitchen facilities already, or in a restaurant or hotel which provide all the necessary services including a room where the bride can change into her going away outfit.

The modern house is generally too small in which to entertain more than a limited number of guests, and rarely big enough to accommodate all those who expect and feel entitled to be invited.

This can be overcome by hiring a marquee or lean-to awning to extend the space available and these normally come in widths of 20, 30 and 40 feet in length. Many firms provide coloured roof and wall linings complete with chandeliers, wall bracket lights or spot lights, and both matting and wooden flooring are available. Such firms will also provide chairs and tables and a range of heaters, should the wedding be during the cold months. (It is becoming increasingly common for families who have hired a marquee to hold a reception followed by a disco in the evening.)

If the bride's mother is a good and highly organised cook it is quite possible for her to prepare and freeze food beforehand and she will need to choose items that can be served easily so that she is not trying to be cook, waitress and hostess on the day. She will also have to hire or borrow enough chairs, small tables, china and cutlery, and organise a wine waiter or two, perhaps from the local off-licence who will be supplying the wine and glasses. Alternatively, a firm of caterers can be brought in who will suggest suitable menus, provide the linen, china and silver as well as serving the food and clearing up afterwards. Most caterers will also serve and deal with the drinks even if they have not provided the wine or the glasses. The bride's mother will also have to organise the flowers and table decorations or arrange for the caterers to take on this responsibility.

If the house is large enough, a room should be set aside for the display of the wedding presents as this gives guests the opportunity to inspect the presents and provides a 'quiet' room away from most of the bustle for the two families to get to know one another better.

The hall will be needed as a reception room where the host and hostess can receive and welcome their guests. The bride's brother and sisters, the bridesmaids and the best man should be briefed to keep the flow of guests passing beyond the reception point towards the main room without pause. As they arrive the guests should shake hands with the bride's mother first and then her father. Immediately afterwards they meet the bridegroom's parents followed by the bride and bridegroom, in that order. To prevent any hold-ups everyone should make their greetings brief and save longer conversations until after all the guests have been received. At large weddings this can take a long time so sometimes the reception line is dispensed with, and the guests are received briefly by bride and groom only.

At this point the guests will be offered a drink – sherry, still or sparkling white wine, with apple, grape or orange juice for those who want it – and they will circulate until the bride and bridegroom make a move towards the buffet table, or, if it is to be a sit down meal, to their places at the top table (see Fig. 4). When the bride and groom have been served or served themselves from the table, it is the general signal for everyone else to do so and they can then either circulate with their food, or take it to a table and join other guests in an informal way.

Where a luncheon or other meal is to be served, the bride and bridegroom sit at the head of the table, the bride on her husband's left. The bride's mother sits next to the bridegroom and the bridegroom's mother on the left of the bride's father who sits next to his newly-married daughter. The best man and the chief bridesmaid complete the top table as shown in Fig. 4.

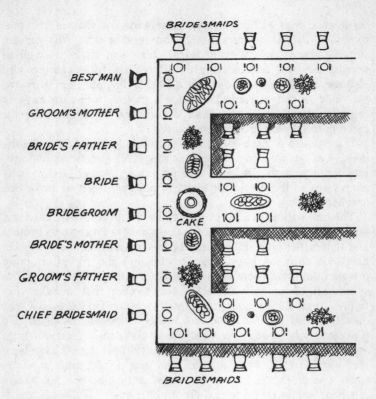

4. The top table.

Alternatively, the best man and chief bridesmaid can take places beside the bride and groom, with the parents further out from the centre, in which case the table would look like Fig. 5. If the groom's parents and bride's parents prefer to sit each beside their own partners, then this can be accommodated with the layout of Fig. 6.

Depending on the spaces available, the caterer will suggest how the tables and chairs can best be placed so that all those who wish to sit down can do so. Where there is to be a 'serve yourself' buffet, the cake and the bride's bouquet are put at one end, and the bride and groom will stand to one side of the cake during the speeches and toasts.

If the reception is held in a village hall, town hall or other

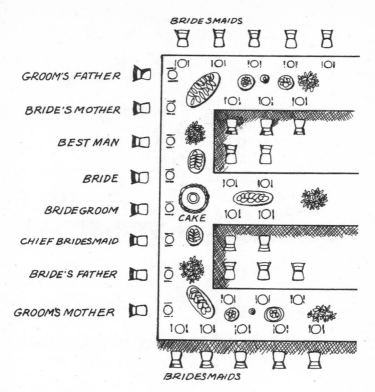

5. Alternative top table.

rooms, an area needs to be kept clear in which the guests are greeted and here again a caterer will be able to suggest the best way of arranging the room or rooms.

Most medium and large hotels have the facilities and often specialise in the organisation of wedding receptions. Their staff will cook and serve almost any meal desired; they will provide the wines and give advice on the subject; they will arrange the tables, the decorations, cloakrooms, the reception room, the dining room, and, if required, a room for the display of the wedding presents.

Their commissionaire, or doorman, should be outside on the pavement ready to open car doors – and to keep a space free of parked vehicles immediately opposite the entrance.

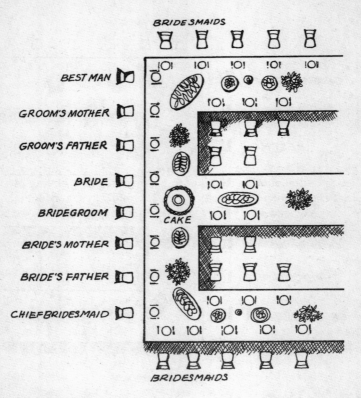

6. Another alternative.

The hall porter will be ready to direct the guests to the apartments allocated for the function and the cloakroom attendants ready to receive the coats.

Sherry, white wine (or champagne) and non-alcoholic fruit juices will be poured into glasses ready to be served as the guests arrive and the waitresses briefed to move among them with trays prepared and loaded with the reception drinks.

Arrangements for all receptions need to be made well in advance. The host and hostess will have to decide on the following:

(a) The time and date.
(b) The menu.

(c) The wines and soft drinks to be served.

(d) Who is to make and ice the cake?

(e) What flowers are to be used on the tables and who provides them?

(f) The number of guests to be present.

(g) The seating plan, if one is needed.

(h) Whether they require a room in which the bride can change into her going away outfit.

A reception after the wedding ceremony is intended to allow the guests to congratulate the newly-weds, to join in the toasts to the health and happiness of the couple, to witness the cutting of the cake and to wish them well as they leave for their honeymoon. It is also an opportunity for the two families to get to know each other better.

The meal itself is incidental to the celebrations and is served because the guests will be hungry long before the bride and bridegroom leave for their honeymoon – especially if they have travelled any distance to attend the wedding. As the meal has always been an essential need, it has long been the custom to use it for the high-spot feature of the celebrations. During it, the toasts are given, the cake cut and the greetings messages read to the guests. Because of this, all the arrangements need a great deal of thought and careful planning.

There are many methods and fashions in which to conduct a ceremonial wedding breakfast and/or evening reception. Few of the arrangements are obligatory, though custom lays down certain broad highlights. The main thing to remember is that it is the day of the newly-weds.

Advance Arrangements

The wedding cake

The cake must be ordered many weeks in advance of the wedding and apart from the style and decorations, its size should be considered in relation to the number of guests expected to attend the reception and those who will expect to receive a portion who were unable to be present. It is quite common for the cake to be home-made and professionally iced. It should be delivered to the caterer at the reception rooms in good time – either the night before or early on the wedding day itself.

The flowers

Flower arrangements may be part of the package that the caterer offers. If not, the caterer will be glad to receive the flowers that have been ordered by the bride's mother for the tables as early as possible on the morning of the reception. Besides flowers for the tables, one or two large arrangements may be necessary and a florist will always provide these if the family has no good 'flower arranging' friends. If a posy is required for the top of the wedding cake this can also be provided by the florist.

Menus and other printed material

Details of the menus and wines will have been settled weeks in advance of the wedding date between the hosts and the caterer or hotelier. If menus are required these should be ordered and printed then (although a hotel may provide these as part of a wedding reception package), along with paper serviettes with the names or initials of the bride and bridegroom, place cards, drink mats, ash trays and book matches, as required. Samples of these items can be seen at any large stationers and can be ordered through them to meet individual requirements. Whatever is ordered should be in the hands of the caterer the day before the wedding – not forgetting the need to write the guests' names on the place cards.

The reception rooms

Although the rooms required for the reception will have been agreed with the caterer and booked some time in advance there are still a few arrangements which must be completed by the host. If a hall has been hired, it is as well to check with the caretaker that the hall will have been cleaned the day before, that there are adequate tables and chairs, whether or not the hall provides towels and soap in the cloakrooms and whether the hall has its own flower vases for larger arrangements.

If the wedding presents are to be displayed the caterer will need to know how many trestle tables will be required and if a separate room is used it should be cleared of unnecessary furniture. On the afternoon before the wedding the bride's parents, the bride and bridegroom and possibly the best man will make a display of the gifts, making sure to keep the wrappings and boxes so that they can be transported safely after the wedding reception.

If the presents are valuable, they should be insured to include their display. A hotelier will do his best to safeguard them overnight and during the reception, but he is unlikely to accept responsibility for theft or damage; caterers coming into a hall booked by the hosts will take no responsibility for them whatsoever. The room should be locked overnight and unlocked as the guests are due to arrive. It is up to the bridal party to remove the presents afterwards (see page 89).

The seating arrangements

The caterer will need to have a general idea of how many guests are to be entertained some time in advance of the event – and he should be given final details, together with the seating plan and the place-cards, not later than the evening before the wedding. There are certain formalities concerning the seating arrangements, though a hostess should not distress herself if she finds it more convenient, or a happier solution, to seat people in some other manner. This plan cannot be made without the assistance of the caterer who will advise on the layout of the tables to suit the numbers involved, the shape and style of the room and the service points.

The top table is the most important and the main preoccupation of the planner, and the simplest arrangements are those already given on page 120. So far as other guests are concerned, brothers and sisters should be interspersed by their wives and husbands (where applicable). Uncles and aunts follow and then the friends of the newly-weds. The length of the side tables will depend largely on the size and shape of the room and the number of guests to be seated.

If there is plenty of room, only the outer sides should be used so that everybody has a clear view of everybody else. Usually this is impracticable – or it would make the tables stretch out to such a length that those towards the foot of each arm will be out of touch with the top table. In such case the inner sides of the arms should be used.

Under no circumstances should the inner side of the top table be used for seating purposes. The cake, on a small separate table in front of the bridal couple, should be the only thing to screen their faces. Even this is often placed to one corner of the room.

Of course, even larger layouts may be used, and for numbers in excess of, perhaps, 200, an attractive arrangement can be made with separate tables set at an angle to the top table, so that not one of the guests will have their backs fully turned towards the newly-weds. (Fewer guests in a small room can also be accommodated in this way.) This plan can be extended to suit the room, either by adding extra sprigs if the room is long, or by lengthening them if it is broad. However, the caterer will have expert knowledge and his advice should be sought.

The variety of possible seating arrangements for the guests is almost infinite, depending on whether the meal is a self-service buffet or a waitress-served sit-down meal. A buffet can be completely informal, with guests eating on the move or sitting anywhere at tables or simply on chairs provided; or a seating plan can be given, with everyone allocated a specific place to sit, as would happen for a sit-down, waitress served meal. However the guests are seated, the one thing that must happen is that the bridal party will have a table, known as the 'top table' at which to sit. This will face the guests and may well display the wedding cake too.

After due consideration has been given to the arrangement for seating the members of the two families, their husbands and wives, and the friends of the bride and bridegroom, an attempt should be made to alternate the sexes as far as possible. A good hostess will also give thought to the problem of family feuds, jealousies and friendships. Such likes and dislikes, if they are not sorted out before the reception, may well lead to quarrels, unhappy silences and outspoken comments. To separate anti-pathetic guests, irrespective of their seating 'rights', is much better than to leave matters to take their course and hope for the best. This is the newly-weds' 'day' and every effort must be made to keep it free of friction. 'Off-beat' guests might well be kept at a distance from the top table, humorists kept apart and younger couples with a personal interest in one another placed happily side-by-side.

The suggestion is that the bride's family and friends should occupy the tables on the bridegroom's side of the room – and vice versa, but others will persuade the host and hostess that the families should be mixed as freely as possible. Both arrangements have a lot to commend them to the hostess. Mixing the families does tend to give them an opportunity to get to know one another, while segregation may mean less embarrassment to all concerned.

The table plan, with places marked with the name of a guest, should be given to the caterer to post up in a convenient place so that the guests will be able to go straight to their places as they enter the dining room – and confirm the actual seat by means of the place-card bearing his or her name lying on the table by the place.

The Arrival

Though the newly-weds leave the church first, it is important that the bride's parents arrive first at the reception. As host and hostess they must be the first to greet their guests as they arrive, if there is to be a reception line.

The reception line should consist of:

The bride's mother
The bride's father
The bridegroom's mother
The bridegroom's father
The bride
The bridegroom

in that order.

If the reception is to include a buffet meal, the official greeting by both sets of parents and the newly-weds almost invariably takes place immediately on the arrival of the guests, but if there is to be a luncheon, it is quite usual for this greeting of the guests to take place later, as they pass into the dining room.

This is often preferred as it relieves the parents and the newly-weds of the duty to rush to the reception rooms from the ceremony and gives the bride time to recover composure. It also enables the photographer to take his pictures of the cutting of the cake while the guests remove their coats and prepare themselves to meet other guests before passing along the reception line.

Assume that the official greeting is to take place immediately on the arrival of the guests: in this case, guests are welcomed by their hosts and the bridal couple as they arrive – without regard to family seniority. The greetings must be brief if there is not to be a long line of impatiently waiting guests and the best man and bridesmaids should do their best to move them on by directing them towards the already poured drinks.

They should be encouraged, too, to circulate about the room, to meet one another – and, of course, take the opportunity to inspect the wedding presents.

The guests should arrive as promptly as possible so that the bridal party can finish with the greetings and then lead the guests towards the meal.

The Wedding Meal

As soon as the last guest has been received, the best man should lead the couple and other members of the bridal party to where their guests are conversing and enjoying a drink. They may join them for a while but must avoid standing in cliques and not allow any one person to monopolise their attention.

They may spend a few minutes inspecting their wedding presents and discussing them with their guests – but the best man must keep his eye on the time.

As soon as the caterer or one of his staff indicates that the meal is ready, he should persuade the newly-weds to move towards the tables arm-in-arm. Behind the newly-weds, the bridal party should be in the following order:

The bride's father with the bridegroom's mother.
The bridegroom's father with the bride's mother.
The best man with the chief bridesmaid.
The bridesmaids.
The pages.

And, finally, the guests.

Before entering the dining room the guests should have examined the seating plan and so, with the help of the place-cards, should have little difficulty in locating their seats.

When everybody has found his or her place, the best man should obtain silence and if 'grace' is to be said, call upon the clergyman or minister present to 'say grace'. Often, in the absence of a clergyman or minister, a known member of a church among the guests may be invited to do this duty but he or she should be approached in advance, not on the day itself. Failing any of these arrangements the task should be undertaken by the bride's father. One of the following forms of words would be suitable:

(a) *For our families, our friends and for this food which you give us, we thank you Lord.*

(b) *Receive our thanks, O Lord, for this food and for this happy day.*

(c) *We thank you, our Father, for good food which brings health, and human love which brings happiness.*

(d) *For what we are about to receive, may the Lord make us truly thankful and ever mindful of the needs of others.*

Grace is often neglected nowadays, and may not be appropriate at a reception following a civil wedding. However, after a church wedding if a minister of religion is present the grace should never be omitted.

The Speeches
As soon as the guests appear to have reached the end of their meal, the toasts are drunk. Unless an official toastmaster is present the best man takes on this role and calls on the first speaker when he thinks the time is ripe.

The bride's father
The first speech is given either by a close personal friend or by a relative of the bride – usually her father. The toast is: 'The Health and Happiness of the Bride and Bridegroom'.

Though it is usual for this toast to be given by the bride's father – or guardian – it is not uncommon for that duty to be passed to some other male member of the bride's family who is deemed to be perhaps a better speaker or is someone of note. But the bride's father must remember to delegate such a task some days in advance and not spring it on an unsuspecting guest at the last moment.

The speech is usually of a semi-serious nature, especially if it is made by the father and generally includes:

1. The happiness he and his wife have experienced in bringing up their daughter, the treasure she has been to them and the loss they will feel following her marriage and move to a home of her own.
2. A couple of interludes in her life – one perhaps amusing, the other more serious.
3. A welcome into the family to the new son-in-law and an

129

expression of the hope that it will be gaining a son rather than losing a daughter.

4. A welcome, too, to the bridegroom's parents.
5. Perhaps an episode concerning the bride and the bridegroom together – particularly if they have known one another for a number of years.
6. A little timely advice to the newly-weds, usually bound up with his own experiences in company with his wife – the bride's mother.
7. The toast to the Health and Happiness of the couple.

Of course, this is merely a suggestion and it is probable that the proposer will have other things to say and other points to make but he must make his speech with one eye on the clock – and the faces of his guests. The newly-weds may have a plane to catch and guests are easily bored by a lengthy speech.

The bridegroom
The bridegroom then replies on behalf of his wife and himself, thanking the gathering for their good wishes and gifts; their parents for being their parents and all those who have helped to make the wedding ceremony and the reception a success – concluding with the bridesmaids, and in so doing proposes a toast to 'The bridesmaids'.

In the first part, responding to the toast proposed by the bride's father (or whoever has made it), the bridegroom might refer to:

1. The kindness of his parents during his boyhood, their care and attention to his upbringing.
2. The thanks he owes them for his start in life – and for any particular sacrifices they have made on his behalf.
3. A tribute to his wife's parents and anything they may have provided for the couple's future.
4. Perhaps a short episode of his meeting with his bride, of their engagement, difficulties or fortunes.
5. His intention to devote himself to the happiness of his bride.
   At this point the bridegroom may turn his attention to lighter matters and his toast to the bridesmaids, with perhaps:
6. Thanks to his best man for his assistance and possible nuisance value.

7.   A reference to the beauty of the bridesmaids and his thanks for their help during the service.

It is common practice for the bridegroom to present each of the bridesmaids with a small present during his speech (or the bride may do this before the wedding). These presents are by no means mandatory and where given they usually comprise some small piece of jewellery, such as a silver chain with a pendant or a locket or a pair of ear-rings. If there are any pages, they should not be overlooked – some sort of toy is generally most suitable for them.

The best man

The best man then responds on behalf of the bridesmaids. His speech should be light and, as far as possible, filled with humour. From this point there should be no return to emotional references or serious topics – and the ability to make such a speech is often taken very much into consideration by the bridegroom when choosing his best man. He might refer to:

1.   The bridegroom's luck in getting the bride he has – and how many another man has wept over her poor choice.
2.   The difficulty in getting a scared bridegroom to the altar.
3.   The joy he and his friends feel at getting rid of him from their bachelor ranks and their pity for an unfortunate bride.
4.   And, of course, the thanks of the bridesmaids for the presents and good wishes they have received from the bridegroom.

(The female best man must be even more tactful than a male best man. If she is a friend of the groom, not a relative, she must avoid giving the impression that she ever wanted to take the bride's place. She may refer – briefly – to her unusual role, perhaps using it as an introduction to an anecdote about the groom's idiosyncrasies. Otherwise the usual guidelines for a best man still apply.)

Other speeches

Those three speeches compose the traditional toasts and replies customary at a wedding reception. No further speeches need be given and, as often as not, they are considered sufficient – but it is by no means uncommon, where time permits, for other guests to speak. One most frequently favoured is a speech of thanks to the host and hostess, given usually by some relative of the bridegroom – followed by a reply from the bride's father, very briefly if he has already spoken.

Other speeches are permissible though the greatest need is to avoid boredom, particularly by insincere guests who like the sound of their own voices or who cannot bear not to have taken some noteworthy part in the proceedings.

With one eye on the time, the best man brings the speeches to an end by rising to read the messages of congratulations and good wishes that have arrived for the newly-weds. In reading them he should endeavour to introduce a few light, background comments on the contents and about those who have sent them. The reading of a large number of telemessages can soon become boring as they are usually repetitions and many of the names will be known to few of the guests.

The best man should remember to hand the telemessages to the bride's mother immediately after the reception to be kept until the bride's return from her honeymoon. It is her duty to write and acknowledge them as soon as possible afterwards – generally at the same time as she writes her thanks to those who have sent presents.

The Cake
The ceremony of cutting the cake either follows the speeches or takes place before them to allow the caterers to remove it and slice it, ready for handing round with the coffee. The bride should place the point of the knife near the centre of the bottom tier of the cake. The bridegroom places a hand over his wife's and slowly and carefully helps her to force the point of the blade down into the heart of the cake and then to draw the blade forwards and downwards. They may cut a complete slice and share it between them, but due to the elaborate decorations on many cakes, the inexperience of the couple, and the probable nervousness of the bride, they rarely make more than a token cut.

Usually that completes the formal 'cutting' of the cake. The caterer takes over from that point and, after dismantling the tiers and ornaments, uses his experience to divide up a tier or two of the cake into handy, not over-large portions which the brides-maids can help to distribute amongst the guests. If there is a large number of guests, the catering staff will do the distribution.

The remainder of the cake will be set aside for eventual

distribution to friends and relatives of the newly-weds who have been unable to attend the wedding and the reception afterwards.

It is traditional for the bridesmaids to keep their slices of cake and to place them under their pillows that night – in the belief that they will then dream of their own future husbands.

An Evening Reception

If an evening reception is planned there is often a lull between the wedding breakfast and the arrival of the extra guests in the evening. The hotel or caterers will need to clear the tables from the centre of the room and rearrange them around the edges unless a completely separate room is available for the evening reception. Some guests who have been at the wedding celebrations all afternoon may choose to leave before the evening party gets underway and the bridal couple should be sure to make themselves available to say goodbye to their guests as they leave. Other guests who live close to the reception may take the opportunity to go home for a short while, perhaps to change for the evening.

As the evening guests arrive they will wish to give their congratulations to the newly-weds and to see the bride in her finery. They may well arrive with presents which will need to be stored safely out of harm's way and will want the chance to see any gifts which have already been unwrapped and put on display (see page 89).

Entertainment for the evening usually takes the form of a live band or disco and it is usual for the newly-weds to launch the proceedings with the first dance. An impressive sight can be caused by a couple who have gone to ballroom dance classes in the weeks or months before their wedding to learn steps with which they can sweep across the floor – to the amazement and delight of both friends and family – although the band or disc jockey will need to be warned in advance if a specific piece of music will be wanted. Alternatively, a slow dance could be chosen and other guests could be encouraged to join in as soon as possible if either of the bridal couple are not happy to be the focus of attention on the dance floor. However, it is unlikely that the tradition of the first dance can be avoided altogether!

Food will have to be provided for the evening and the caterer or hotelier will be able to advise on a suitable menu. This usually takes the form of a self-service buffet and is much more informal

133

than the wedding breakfast, with people helping themselves as and when they wish and sitting wherever they choose to eat. If there is still a tier of the wedding cake which has not been cut this could also be displayed on the buffet table and slices can be provided with coffee for those guests who were not at the wedding breakfast if there is enough to go around.

The Departure

Towards the end of the reception the bride retires to change from her wedding finery into her going-away clothes. As she mounts the stairs to the room set aside for this purpose, it is traditional for the bridesmaids to gather at the foot or below the banisters – while the rest of the wedding party stands by to watch the fun.

From a convenient place on the stairs, the bride throws her bouquet to the young ladies gathered below – and the bridesmaid who catches the bouquet can, reputedly, expect to be the next bride. Or she throws her bouquet as she gets into the car to drive away, in a shower of confetti.

While she changes, her baggage is put with the bridegroom's at the exit, all ready to load into the car or taxi that is to take the pair of them on the first stage of their honeymoon.

The bridegroom, if he lives near the venue of the reception (or if one of his friends lives nearby) hurries off with his best man to change into his own going-away clothes. If this is not possible, the bridegroom usually finds a convenient spot among the reception rooms – and as his own dressing should take very much less time than that of his wife, he should be all ready and waiting when she comes down the stairs.

While he is waiting, the bridegroom collects from his best man the rail or air tickets and any other travel documents that he needs for the honeymoon.

(It is often at this time that the young friends of the bridal couple sneak out to 'decorate' the going away car with tin cans, balloons and streamers. Whilst this is considered an essential part of the celebrations by many, it should not be allowed to get out of hand and no damage should be caused to the car.)

When the bride is ready, no further time should be wasted in which emotional scenes may arise. In the years long gone by, partings of this nature were a much more final farewell than they are today. A bride's departure with her husband might have meant a separation for years between her and her parents – sometimes, if they were going abroad, perhaps for ever. Tears and sorrow were natural under such circumstances but modern travel has put the distant parts of the world within a few short hours of home and, with our present standards of living, it is not likely to be impossible for a young couple to save enough for a visit to their parents once in a while. The occasion should therefore be joyful and a mother's inevitable tears kept from sight.

The farewells should be brisk, cheery and smiling. A new and growing custom is for the groom to present his mother and mother-in-law with bouquets of flowers as they say goodbye (although some couples prefer to do this during the groom's speech).

Only after the newly-weds have finally departed for their honeymoon should the guests begin to leave – saying their final goodbyes to the host and hostess (usually the bride's mother and father). Eventually only the hosts and the best man remain behind to clear up the paraphernalia of presents, clothes, wedding cake – and the odds and ends that will surely be forgotten by their owners.

18

After The Show

Before leaving the reception rooms the bride's mother should remember to pick up what is left of the wedding cake. Almost certainly the caterer will have packed it in a box strong enough to protect what is left of the sugary confection.

She must also gather up, pack and take away with her the wedding clothes left behind by her daughter – and make certain that none of her lady guests has left anything behind.

At the same time, someone – often the best man – will pack and take away the discarded clothes of the bridegroom and make sure that arrangements have been made for returning any morning suits or other wedding outfits hired by the groom and best man (and perhaps those of the fathers and the ushers if they all came from the same shop). Also, the best man should see to it that nothing has been left behind by any of the male guests and pass to the bride's mother any greetings messages not already handed to the bride.

If the wedding presents have not been unwrapped during the reception these can probably be transported to the bride's mother's home by the bride's family (perhaps with the help of the best man) immediately at the end of the reception. However, if they have been unwrapped and put on display it may be easier to leave them for a few hours or overnight (as long as they will be safely locked away) until someone such as the best man and some helpers can return with boxes, packing cases, paper and string to re-pack the gifts and transport them safely. They can then be displayed at the home of the bride's parents in some little-used room until they are taken to the home of the newly-weds (see page 89).

The bride's mother will settle down to the task of dividing up sufficient of the wedding cake to be able to send a piece to each of the friends and relatives of the bride and bridegroom who were unable to attend the wedding and the reception afterwards – perhaps because of age, infirmity, illness or distance.

The stationers from whom the wedding invitation cards were obtained may provide the tiny boxes in which to pack the segments of cake. A nice touch would be to have cards printed, fitting the boxes, ready to accompany each piece of cake. The wording will probably be as follows, remembering that the address of the sender will be that of the young couple's new home:

Mr & Mrs Peter J Smith
The Bungalow
Esher Meade

With compliments on the occasion of their wedding.

[Date]

The bride's maiden name could be printed at the top left and crossed through by a silver arrow – and, indeed, all the printing on the card could be in embossed silver. However, this will add extra expense to an already costly occasion and a simpler arrangement is to use standard pre-printed cards that often come with the boxes.

No acknowledgement of the receipt of the cake should be expected.

On the same day the bride's mother and father can send an announcement of the wedding to the press, for publication in the 'Marriages' section of the classified advertisement columns (see Chapter 11). The local paper is the ideal medium if both the bride and bridegroom come from the same district; the local paper should be used in each district when the couple come from different parts of the country – and if it should happen that one or other of them was widely known or famous, then publication should be made in one of the national daily newspapers.

The bride's parents are expected to make the announcement – not those of the bridegroom. This should be remembered in the case where the bridegroom lived in a different town from that of his bride. It is still her mother's duty to send the announcement to the paper in that town though it is quite usual for the bridegroom's mother to undertake the task, by mutual agreement.

The bride's father must settle down to the task of paying the bills that will flow in to him. He used to be responsible for the cost of the reception, including everything to do with it: the cake, the bridal gown and the bridesmaids' attire, the meal, the wines, the cars, the flowers – while the bridegroom, or his father, needed to square the much smaller account for the wedding ceremony. Nowadays, many families share the cost more evenly.

A day or so before the newly-weds are due back from their honeymoon, the bride's parents should take all the wedding presents to their daughter's home.

As soon as they return, the bride is expected to start on the task of writing to thank all those who gave her and her husband wedding presents, and to acknowledge the greetings messages. Letters of thanks need to be handwritten; they should neither be printed nor typed, however burdensome the duty.

Finally, the last act of the wedding ceremony and ritual takes place spread over the next three months. It is the newly-weds' duty to entertain their relatives and friends in their new home – a few at a time, of course, unless the new home is a very large one. Both sets of parents should be invited first, after which priority should go to the best man, the bridesmaids and the ushers (though with them, if there is room in the house, other guests may be added). Then comes the general run of relatives and friends and their entertainment should be settled as a matter of convenience and preference by the bride and bridegroom. The problem is the question of the numbers to be invited on each occasion and whether the invitation is to tea, to a cheese and wine party or to dinner.

No mandatory method applies. The couple are at liberty to please themselves – so long as the entertainment is to be in their own house and not outside. On the face of it, maiden aunts will prefer an invitation to tea, the friends and relatives of the same generation as the newly-weds to a cheese and wine party, and the parents and grandparents perhaps to dinner.

No formal, printed invitations need be sent out. Verbal arrangements or perhaps a brief note would be sufficient – and acceptances will be returned in the same manner.

19

Choice Of Menu
For The Reception –
At Home Or Away

Likes and dislikes are so individual where food and drink are concerned that it is only possible to make a few tentative suggestions within the scope of a book of this nature. A glance at the cookery shelves in any bookshop or library shows that the scope is unlimited.

The most important point to consider before deciding on a menu is where the meal is to be cooked and served. However expert the amateur cook, it is highly unlikely that home cooking facilities would match that of a first class restaurant or hotel. Even if the bride's mother has in mind a menu that can easily be dealt with in her own kitchen, she needs to be highly organised to undertake the cooking and serving of such a meal since, as hostess, she should normally never have to leave her guests.

However, it is possible to serve a cold meal which can be prepared in advance, plated and ready to serve from a service table or sideboard. For instance, if the bride's mother wanted to give a finger buffet she could serve any of the following:

Vol-au-vents
Sausage rolls
Curry puffs
Individual quiches

which need to be popped into the oven for ten minutes or so to warm through; plus the following served cold:

Fried chicken drumsticks
Cheese and pineapple on cocktail sticks
Sausages on sticks
Thin strips of fried fish served with a dip
Asparagus rolls
Small sandwiches
Profiteroles filled with cream cheese
Small cakes
Choux buns
Biscuits

On the other hand, if she felt she could cater for a fork buffet with three courses, she might start with:

Savoury mousse or
Pâté or
Stuffed eggs

followed by:

A whole salmon
Chicken or turkey pieces served in a sauce
Cold sliced ham, tongue, beef or turkey served with salads
   such as:

Potato salad
Mixed bean salad
Brown rice with corn salad
Celery, walnut and apple salad

and many others which can be found in any good cookery book. 'Salad' no longer has to mean a lettuce leaf and half a tomato! (It should be remembered that a number of the guests may be vegetarian and therefore plenty of interesting meatless dishes should be included in the menu.)

Fruit salad with cream and meringues
Gateaux

Pavlovas
Eclairs or choux buns
Trifle with cream

followed by tea or coffee.

If the bride's family have called in a caterer they will be offered a choice of menus to fit their purse. A hot meal is only advisable where there are adequate kitchen facilities or the caterer does not have a long journey. The following are typical of the choice available:

No 1
    Assorted sandwiches
    Filled bridge rolls
    Chicken and mushroom vol-au-vents
    Vegetarian vol-au-vents
    Sausage rolls
    Genoese fancies
    Fruit salad and fresh cream
    Coffee

No 2 (fork buffet)
    Cold ham and tongue
    Veal, ham and egg pie
    Vegetarian quiche
    Potato salad
    Russian salad
    Green salad
    Tomato salad
    Rolls and butter
    Sausage rolls
    Cocktail sausages
    Assorted pastries
    Fruit salad and fresh cream
    Coffee

No 3 (sit down meal)
    Soup or
    Orange and grapefruit cocktail
    Rolls and butter

Fillet of Sole Princess
Hot roast chicken with bacon
Mushroom Stroganoff
Buttered new potatoes
Garden peas
Fruit salad and cream
Coffee
Petit fours

No 4 (sit down meal)
Melon cocktail
Smoked salmon with lemon and brown bread
Cold roast turkey with ham
Vegetarian flans
A variety of salads
Croquette or buttered potatoes

Alternatively:
Hot roast turkey with stuffing
Vegetable pilau
Buttered or croquette potatoes
Garden peas

Sherry trifle with cream
Cheese board
Petit fours
Coffee

No 5 (fork buffet)
Lobster or crab mayonnaise
Roast fillet of beef with horseradish sauce
Chicken in cream sauce with pineapple
Stuffed peppers (vegetarian)
Served with green salad and pasta salad
French bread and butter
Lemon soufflé or chocolate gateau
Coffee

No 6 (sit down meal for a summer wedding)
Melon balls or salmon mousse
Roast lamb with mint sauce

Vegetarian stir fry with tofu
Served with hot new potatoes, green salad, kidney beans,
   carrots, fennel, and chicory in herb vinaigrette salad
Strawberries or raspberries and cream
Coffee

If the reception is to be held at a restaurant or hotel, any menu is possible provided the items are available and the hostess is prepared to pay for the meal she envisages. Certainly, hot meals are better in a restaurant or hotel where they have all the facilities on hand and the food can be cooked when required, not hours beforehand then kept warm or re-heated as can happen in a hired hall.

It is usual to offer guests a glass of sherry, white wine or champagne on their arrival at the reception. Increasingly popular is the use of sparkling wines throughout the reception or a still white wine with a good champagne being used for the toasts. As there are often children at weddings as well as those guests who cannot (or do not wish to) drink anything alcoholic, there should always be a good supply of fresh fruit juice, apple and grape juice available and mineral water or perhaps a jug of non-alcoholic fruit punch on each table.

The amount required can be estimated on the basis of six glasses of wine or champagne to each bottle, and the average guest having three to four glasses (or half a bottle of wine) each.

If the reception is to be at home or in a hall, the local wine shop or off-licence can advise on wines and will usually arrange supplies on a sale or return basis. They will often also lend glasses. In a hotel or restaurant, the manager will suggest which wines he has in his cellar and which are the most suitable. They will normally charge for the bottles actually opened.

Many people who are hosting the reception at home or in a hired hall take the opportunity now available to go abroad and get the wine (and perhaps beers) at duty free prices. This can work out cheaper for the alcohol but against this has to be balanced the cost of getting there, transporting the purchases home, and all the extra work involved. Even where this has been done it might still be worth getting some wine from the local off-licence on a sale or return basis to make sure that there is no danger of running out!

Champagnes, white wines and sherries should be chilled – two or three hours in cold water will help where no ice or other coolant is available. Red wines should be served at room temperature by being left on the dining room sideboard for an hour or more before they are to be served. Bottles of red wine should be uncorked about an hour before being served to allow the contents to 'breathe'.

If more than one wine is to be served, remember that dry white wines should be drunk before both red wines and sweet wines, and that younger wines should always be served before older ones.

20

Silver and Golden Weddings

Wedding anniversaries have always been regarded as a purely private occasion between a man and his wife – except on the rare days when the 'silver' or 'golden' weddings come around. Other than those, the anniversaries are usually celebrated with a private party *à deux*, in whichever way the couple choose: a day out, a meal in a restaurant followed by a visit to the theatre, or perhaps a dinner dance or trip to a night club, and often an eternity ring to mark the first anniversary.

As the years go by, the couple tend to gather about themselves a family and the regular celebrations tend to become a thing of the past. Forgotten perhaps; often made impracticable by the demands of babies. Even then many couples try and mark the day in at least some way: an exchange of small presents and perhaps something special for dinner, including a bottle of wine, or perhaps a meal out.

The years slide past and the couple begin to become so absorbed in a welter of such events as children's birthdays, Christmas Days, the school holidays and, in time, their children's own wedding days, that suddenly – almost unbelievably – they find the day approaching when they have completed a quarter of a century of married life. Their Silver Wedding Day.

Something special is called for. First, an announcement in the press, sent by the couple themselves, might read:

SMITH-JONES – on 20 April [date] at St George's Parish Church, Woodhouse, Peter John Smith to Ann Jones. Present address: The Bungalow, Esher Meade.

Secondly, they will exchange gifts and may expect to receive presents from their family and close friends. Where possible, the presents should consist of silver articles, or where this is not feasible because of cost – particularly in the case of gifts from children and grandchildren – the gift should be tied into a parcel with silver ribbon (or using silver paper).

The couple may decide to entertain their children, close friends and, wherever possible, the long ago best man and chief bridesmaid at a small party. Formal invitations are not necessary, but they should be issued well in advance so that those who are to be invited may be given time to make their own arrangements.

Formal wear is not usual except in families where it is customary to attend and dress for functions. The venue can be a hotel or a restaurant and is generally arranged in advance so that a small private room may be reserved for the occasion, or (more often) it is held at home.

A wedding cake usually graces the occasion and, following the meal, it is cut in the same token fashion as applied on the occasion of the wedding itself, twenty-five years earlier.

Speeches are usually few and happy. The eldest son might propose the 'Health and Happiness' of his parents and the husband should reply on behalf of his wife and himself. Other speeches may follow – almost entirely composed of reminiscences – from the best man or one of the guests who was present at the wedding.

The party may move on to a theatre or a dance.

Another quarter of a century may go by and then comes the grand occasion of the Golden Wedding. This time the small party to celebrate the event is usually organised by the eldest son of the couple – often in consultation with his brothers and sisters. He will make the announcement public through the press, in similar fashion to that published twenty-five years before.

On this occasion the presents should be of gold, though very often they are much less valuable and merely tied up with gold coloured ribbon, or wrapped in gold coloured paper.

Again, the party can be held at a hotel or restaurant if at all possible and equally, if possible, the guests of twenty-five years previously should be invited once again – together with the rising generation of grandchildren. Often one of the daughters may arrange the party, do the catering, and hold it in her home.

No formal dress is required, nor need any official invitations be sent out. A cake is usual, though not obligatory.

After the cutting of the cake there may be a few informal speeches but the husband is not compelled to reply in person. Sometimes one of the young grandchildren present performs this office for him – though there is no set order of precedence involved. It is unusual for any sort of entertainment to follow.

At the end of the party it is customary for the eldest son and his wife to escort his parents home. They do not stay when they arrive and none of the guests should follow.

The Diamond Wedding follows on the sixtieth anniversary of their wedding day and follows very much the same lines as the celebrations for the Golden Wedding. However, the presents almost never consist of diamonds and rarely of anything of more intrinsic value than flowers.

The family party should be kept as small as possible and, because of the age of the couple, is usually held either in their own home, or that of one of their children.

The wedding cake need only be a token and, as on previous anniversaries, there is no need for pieces of it to be distributed to absent friends and relatives.

The whole celebration must be geared to the ability of the couple to stand up to the fuss – and, again, the eldest son and his wife should bring the proceedings to a close as soon as tiredness begins to dull the pleasure of the couple.

As a matter of interest, though of little moment today, anniversaries of a wedding are traditionally known as:

1st anniversary	Paper
2nd anniversary	Cotton
3rd anniversary	Leather
4th anniversary	Silk
5th anniversary	Wood
6th anniversary	Iron
7th anniversary	Wool
8th anniversary	Bronze
9th anniversary	Pottery
10th anniversary	Tin
12th anniversary	Linen
15th anniversary	Crystal
20th anniversary	China
25th anniversary	SILVER

30th anniversary ....Pearl or Ivory
35th anniversary...Coral
40th anniversary ....Ruby
45th anniversary ....Sapphire
50th anniversary..GOLD
55th anniversary ....Emerald
60th anniversary ....DIAMOND
75th anniversary................................and again, DIAMOND

Part Two
Speeches

21

A Word About Speeches

A wedding is an occasion that should be enjoyed by all – even those giving the speeches! But many called on to make a speech at these times have never spoken to a gathering before and the thought of standing in front of a group of people often fills them with horror. To overcome this there are 46 example speeches gathered here. Amongst these there is bound to be one that suits the wedding at which you are to speak – whether it's the first wedding of a young couple or the 'second-time around' for two people with adult children.

There are example speeches for the three traditional wedding speakers – the bride's father, the bridegroom and the best man – plus speeches that members of the bride's family could give in her father's place if necessary. Beyond those usual three, it is becoming increasingly common for others to have a say, including the ladies. So among the extra speeches at the end are some which could be given by the bride herself or her sister or mother.

Every speech is a complete entity. However, to suit an individual situation each speech can be adapted and have incorporated into it appropriate material from any of the other speeches.

It's a good idea for all those who are to speak at the wedding to confer in advance and make sure they are not duplicating material or using the same jokes! In fact some pairs of speeches are included here which can be used together: see pages 175 and 279, 178 and 254, and 181 and 229.

When a speech is composed, the feelings of the people who are being talked about must be considered; nothing should be said which could be misinterpreted (unless that is the deliberate intention) and no-one should be ridiculed to such an extent that they are hurt by the words. A speech should make everyone laugh – including the person who is the butt of the jokes!

How to deliver the speech

After you're compiled your speech, make clear notes large enough to be read at a quick glance without the need to keep bending down if they are lying face up on a table.

Rehearse out loud facing a mirror. This will give you confidence and the required practice in the proper form of delivery for each part of the speech, including cheerful looks and smiles in the appropriate places. Stand up straight and look around your imagined audience so that this will come easily during the delivery and you will be able to concentrate on putting life into the speech itself.

If time is too short for you to learn your speech (using merely guiding notes) and you are obliged to read it all out, then you will have to write it all out in a formal way, differently from the free-and-easy spontaneity of manner used in this book. If you do write your whole speech out, leave ample space between the lines to make it easy to follow and save you from losing your place.

Above all, don't worry about your speech; you're giving it at a wedding and your audience is bound to be good-natured – many of them will have been in a similar position and will sympathise with any nerves you might have.

The best man often acts as toastmaster at the wedding reception and he calls on the first speaker when he considers the time is right. The traditional order of speeches at the reception is:

1. The bride's father – at the end of his speech he toasts the health and happiness of the bride and groom.
2. The bridegroom – replies on behalf of his wife and himself and, at the end of his speech, toasts the bridesmaids.

3. The best man – replies on the bridesmaids' behalf. If there are any telemessages or cards from absent family or friends, he will read these out at the end of his speech.

4. If any others are going to speak, they would usually speak now; then 'the cutting of the cake' may follow (if it didn't take place before the speeches).

22

Bride's Father's Speeches

Bride's Father No. 1

Whenever I've been thinking aloud about what I'd like to say on this happy occasion, the wife has kept chipping in with, 'Don't forget to thank everybody for coming.' There am I, trying to work out something grandiose to fasten your attention on my every word, and Mary has to deflate my mood with (MOCKINGLY) 'Don't forget to thank everybody for coming!' I can't imagine that Winston Churchill had that trouble when he was preparing one of his important speeches to Parliament. Fancy him having to say, 'Thank you all for coming,' to satisfy Mrs Churchill. Anyway, to save myself getting into trouble, thank you all for coming.

Of course my thanks would have been there even if I had overlooked to express them. It's lovely to be surrounded by family and friends at the same time, and to bask in the atmosphere of an event like this. Weddings are invariably very happy occasions, and this one is no exception.

Having thanked you all for being here, I'd like to say a special 'thank you' to John. Yes, I do refer to Jane's John. You see, it is not only Jane and John's day, but Mary's and mine too, because we have gained as a son someone of whom we are greatly fond, and both of us are so grateful to him for coming here as the bridegroom.

With our other children we had to do things like forever changing nappies, and getting up in the night to find out why they were crying, and when they were a little older buy them ice creams to shut them up. With John we haven't had to change a single nappy. He's come to us as a young man ready-made.

I don't like the mouthful 'son-in-law'. It sounds as though 'son' is qualified and the person concerned is a step away. Certainly for Mary and myself the 'in-law' tag is merely legal terminology irrelevant to the relationship between John and ourselves. What makes things so much more joyful for us is knowing that our dear Jane has this young man as a husband. In the nicest way we can say that they deserve each other.

What we find gratifying also is that John's parents feel the same about Jane. They have taken her to their hearts and they must now feel that they have gained a lovely daughter.

With such all-round harmony we feel thrice blessed ... I don't think I've ever said that before – 'thrice'. It's surprising what you come out with in a speech ... It sounds as if we've had triplets.

A word of caution to the bridegroom, however, will not go amiss. As an old married man – well, it can make you feel old, even if you are only middle-aged – I can speak from experience to this freshman here and warn him what he'll be up against. I didn't think it wise to say anything before he'd gone through the wedding ceremony, in case he changed his mind. There's something you'll have to learn to live with, John, because no man has yet found a remedy for it, and that is the unfathomable female mind. It can be summed up by one simple instance.

A woman bought her husband two ties for his birthday, a red one and a blue one. He was undecided which one to wear at his party that evening, but he appeared in the red one. As soon as his wife saw him she said, 'Oh, you're wearing the red tie. Don't you like the blue one?'

There's no way you can win. However, forewarned is fore-armed and now John is forearmed, in that at least he knows what to expect.

Don't worry too much, John. Mary and I have known Jane for a lot longer than you have, and things shouldn't be quite as bad as that. In any case, with your resourcefulness you would probably do something like wearing two ties at the same time. I've done stranger things than that to keep the peace with Mary, but if you and Jane have half the happiness in your married life that we have had in ours, then yours will be a very happy marriage indeed.

It is my pleasure to ask everyone to drink to that.

Ladies and gentlemen, would you please join me in a toast to the health and happiness of Jane and John.

(IMMEDIATELY AFTER THE TOAST) Oh, and by the way, just to make doubly sure, thank you all for coming.

Bride's Father No. 2
(Bride a waitress)

Well, here we go again. This is the third wedding speech I've made. At the first of them the bridegroom was one of the most handsome you could wish to see. His bride must have been the envy of all the ladies that set eyes on him. She surely was a very lucky lady. That young man has not lost any of his charm with the passing years. But that's enough about me.

The second wedding was that of one of our daughters. Now it is another daughter, so this is my second speech as the bride's father.

There are three ladies in my life that I am proud of and who are a source of immense happiness to me. The firstcomer was Mary. The second to appear was our dear daughter, Joan, and the third was another dear daughter, our Jane, today's bride.

One thing leads to another, and that's certainly true of a wedding. The wedding of Mary and myself has led to two more weddings already. All three weddings have had one thing in common for me. The feeling of pride that I had at my own wedding came back to me when Joan was married, and it's come back again today.

Until Joan married we didn't have a son, but we gained one in Alan. It was as though our family had suddenly increased. Now the same thing is happening again. We're gaining another son.

When it was just the two of us, Mary and myself, I felt outnumbered. A man does, you know. In any argument (and I do mean friendly argument, not a quarrel) between man and wife, the man does feel outnumbered, because the wife says twice as much as the man. (John, I hope you're listening carefully. This is being explained for your benefit.) Now, the reason that the wife says twice as much as the man is because the wife carries on talking while the man is silently trying to fathom the logic of the statements that she's just made. It dawned on me too late in my married life that all the time I'd spent trying to find that elusive logic had been wasted. There wasn't any logic.

When Joan was old enough to stand on her own verbal feet, the outnumbering ratio was three to one, and when Jane was old enough, it was four to one. With the acquisition of two more males, the balance is tipping in my favour when we're all together.

Mary and I are delighted that Jane, like her sister before her, has made a splendid match. Jane and John have known each other long enough to be able to start their married life together happy in the knowledge that they get on famously together. They're alike in their natures, active and eager to have a go at anything.

When Jane was only in her infancy she took up the violin, and after a few minutes of determined effort we managed to get it off her. What made us do that was not so much the sound of her playing as the sound of Stradivari turning in his grave.

She couldn't wait to take driving lessons. I knuckled under to her persuasion to give her some instruction as soon as she was old enough. Have you ever seen anybody do a three-point turn at 45 miles an hour? Naturally Jane's become more skilful since then. She can now do a three-point turn at 60 miles an hour.

She knew nothing about the requirements of the driving test on that first practice. I said, 'Quick! Do an emergency stop!' She said, 'What's the emergency?' I said, 'I want to get out.'

I've heard it said that some people live by their wits and others by their common sense. Jane lives by both. This gives her the advantage to deal with any crisis. And believe me, in her job as a waitress, from the tales that are told, this is a godsend. When the chef's at fault, it's still the waitress that has to deal with the complaint. She served to one man a bowl of something piled up like a pyramid. When he protested, she pointed out to him that he had asked for the thick soup.

Her resourcefulness has saved the situation many a time. A woman ordered some Emmental cheese. They hadn't any left, so Jane cut a chunk out of cheddar and drilled holes in it.

The menu contained a long list – 'eggs on toast', 'beans on toast', 'cheese on toast', 'sardines on toast', and so on. One day the equipment overheated and Jane added 'toast on fire'.

John, my son, you're going to be in capable hands.

May I say in conclusion that Mary and I are happy to welcome into our fold two nice people not yet mentioned, but without whom John wouldn't be here. No, I don't mean the best man and the taxi driver, but John's parents, already our valued friends.

Ladies and gentlemen, it is my privilege and pleasure finally to propose the toast to the continuing health and happiness of Jane and John.

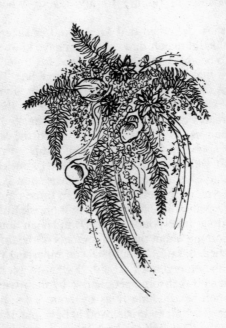

Bride's Father No. 3
(Bride a shop assistant)

In the normal way I should be apprehensive about standing up and making a speech. This occasion, however, is different, and the difference is that there are many thoughts that I am only too eager to express which are, as it were, close to home.

With some speeches that are compulsory we may have to grope for things to say, but a proud and happy father can find his mind overflowing with thoughts on such an occasion as this.

When I settled down to make some notes, putting my thoughts into some sort of order, no end of variety of things popped into my head to convey to you the rich experience that Mary and I have enjoyed in bringing up Jane and having her with us right until today, when she embarks upon life in her own home. Yes, so many things, but don't worry, you're only going to hear a few of them, because this is a wedding reception and not my one-man speech day.

Jane has been a wonderful daughter to Mary and myself and at this point of our parting with her into another's keeping we thank her for all the twenty-one unbroken years of joy that she has given us. I know that she's twenty-three, but we don't count the first two years because then she used to wake us up at all times of the night.

The delightful little girl that we found ourselves with went on to become a delightful big girl with many admirers and many suitors, all but one of whom, of course, were destined to fall by the wayside. With Jane's kind heart she would have done her best to let them down lightly. She's always been a thoughtful girl and she's always been a happy girl. What more could parents ask for, even though Mary and I did get much, much more?

What more, indeed, could the customers who enter her shop ask for in the person who serves them? We all know what a difference it makes when a sales assistant is of a pleasant, friendly disposition and tries to be helpful. It doesn't matter whether you're buying slippers or kippers, the person who serves you either adds to or detracts from the quality of your life for that short while, and it's the Janes of this world that add to the quality of our lives.

I'm reminded of a young lad who started work in a grocer's shop and all he knew about food was that it was something you ate. A regular customer went in on the lad's first day. She'd brought some cheese back and she said to him, 'This smells.' He said, 'It's supposed to,' and she said, 'It's not supposed to smell smelly.' He said, 'Well, leave it with us and we'll see if we can make it better.'

I'm sure that kind of service is a far cry from our Jane's early days behind a counter.

John, to turn to your good self, Jane's mother and I have been on cloud nine ever since you chose us as your mother-in-law and father-in-law. You can relax and rest assured that Jane's mum will not live up to the traditional image of a mother-in-law. I know her too well for that. Just because she slighted you for not letting her chaperone Jane on the honeymoon don't get the wrong impression of how she's going to be in the future.

Ladies and gentlemen, I believe that I'm running out of time, if I'm to allow others to speak, so I'll try to be brief.

I hinted at the start that the wealth of happiness that Jane has given to Mary and myself could not be summed up adequately in a short speech. I have proved myself right. There is, however, something that Mary and I should like emphasised before I finish, and that is that today we honour not Jane alone, whom we can say so much about because we've known her intimately all her life, but also the splendid lad that we have known for only a fraction of that time, namely John.

Furthermore, we wish to say a very warm welcome into the family to John's mum and dad, and indeed all their family.

Now, Jane and John, it is to both of you that we are going to raise our glasses and wish you health and happiness in your future as man and wife.

Ladies and gentlemen, will you please join me in a toast to Jane and John.

Bride's Father No. 4

A wedding is always thought of as a bride and groom's special day, but it's also a special day for their parents, because it's an important event in their own married life.

If it's the first time that one of their offspring is getting married, then it's a milestone. Now, what is a milestone? I suppose we've all seen Dick Whittington in the pantomime. There is Dick, consulting an AA map, trying to work out how much farther it is to London, and there's a giant cat miaowing and pointing a paw at a stone pillar by the wayside, on which is shown the number of miles to go. A milestone marks the point of completion of a certain distance on a journey.

This has become a metaphor for reaching a stage in life or in one of life's undertakings. In Dick Whittington's day a milestone in the literal sense was something that tempted the weary foot-traveller to stop and rest awhile, undo his packed lunch and entertain thoughts of what lay ahead.

Today a milestone has been reached by some of us here, and all of us have sat down and eaten the packed lunch. I hasten to add that I'm still speaking figuratively when I refer to our delicious meal in that way.

For Mary and myself it's the completion of looking after a child of ours under our own roof. We have brought up that child and taken care of her to the best of our ability until she has become mature enough and prepared enough to start her own married life, outside our keeping. So at one and the same time it's a milestone in the lives of Mary and myself on the one hand and of Jane on the other. That's not all of course, because the same situation is reflected in John and his parents.

As we six travellers pause on our journey I suspect that the hearts and minds of Jane and John are too overflowing with joyful thoughts of the married life ahead of them for there to be any room for serious reflection on the past. That's good. It's we other four who look back. Jane and John rejoice because they have just gained each other. We parents have reached the end of that part of our lives during which we had the joy of the close company of our respective children, and our jubilation at today's event can be touched with a sense of loss.

I don't need to expand on that because you will all know what I mean. I mention it only as a tribute to Jane from Mary and myself – a thanks for the immense happiness that it has given us to have her as a daughter.

Now, I took as my text for today the career of Dick Whittington in pantomime. In real life he went on to great prosperity. My life before meeting Mary was more like a pantomime, and this continued in one respect after the milestone of our wedding. I simply changed from Dick Whittington and became Baron Hardup.

My grandmother used to say, 'A penny bun costs you twopence when you're courting.' It didn't cost her twopence. It cost granddad twopence. I discovered that when you've been married a few years and have a family a penny bun could cost you fourpence. Then there was the cat to feed. I suppose I should be grateful that our cat wasn't as big as Dick Whittington's.

Although material prosperity does help to make life a little more comfortable, I am more concerned at this particular time to toast the good fortune of the bride and groom. It is the wish for health and happiness in their married life that I would like us all to keep uppermost in our minds.

Mary and I are truly grateful to all of you for joining us in this happy celebration, and in spite of what I've said about my own plight you needn't put too much money in my hat on your way out – just whatever you can comfortably afford. Really I exaggerated about being Baron Hardup. I've managed to pay for this wedding without strain. It's Jane's sister's wedding that I have to start saving for now. That's why my hat will be there at the door.

So there we are, ladies and gentlemen. That pleasurable moment has arrived when I ask you all to stand and join me in that toast to the health and happiness of bride and groom.

Bride's Father No. 5

(Groom a policeman)

When Mary first told me that Jane and John were serious about each other I was elated. It meant that the burden of the wedding speech that would fall upon me sooner or later would be lightened. Because John was a policeman I should have something to go on.

I started to list all the puns I could think of to do with the police. That was quite a time ago. As that once dreaded moment has arrived when I stand before you guests to start my speech, I have in front of me that list of puns. (PICK UP VERY SMALL PIECE OF PAPER) I've got them written on the back of this receipt I had from Sainsbury's for a jar of onions and two packets of cornflakes.

I thought that would *arrest* your attention. (PICK UP PEN AND CROSS OUT 'ARREST') That's the first one gone. I'll drop the other two out when you don't expect it, so listen for them. Would you believe how difficult it was trying to think of more puns!

Anyway, it would have been comforting for Mary and me to know that the man that Jane was going to marry was a policeman even we hadn't met him, because in our view policemen are solid, reliable and level-headed people and very responsible. They go out there on the streets at all hours of the day and night for our protection and assistance, exposing themselves to abuse and danger.

In the case of young members of the force like John our admiration is heightened, because the dangers that have to be faced are regrettably much greater than a generation ago. It takes courage nowadays to serve the public in the capacity that John has chosen, and the young men – and women – who enter into this deserve our recognition.

This means that the fact alone of John's vocation would be reassuring for Mary and me because of significant things that it would tell us straight away. However, we now know John also as an individual, and everything that we learn about his character first-hand makes us more happy for Jane, to have such a fine partner, and for ourselves, having such a fine son-in-law. (No, 'son-in-*law*' wasn't intentional!)

John is ambitious and is prepared to persevere for promotion, and he has told us that no matter how long it takes, he will *plod* on. (TAKE PAPER AND PEN, CROSS OUT 'PLOD') That's two down and one to go. It was 'plod', for anybody who hadn't noticed.

There's an old saying, 'A policeman's lot is not a nappy one.' Well, Mary and I hope that to some extent it will be, because we like to visualise Jane and John's back garden with a clothesline punctuated with nappies as well as police socks.

One thing, John, if you have as large a family as Mary and I wish on you, there'll be no cause for anxiety. By then you will have had plenty of practice at crowd control. If you forget which one is which, just remember that Jane is (E.G. the tall, fair-haired one who wears glasses).

Jane has never been any trouble to us, John, and I don't think we've been a trouble to her. Isn't that right, Jane? Of course there's always a difficult phase that parents have to endure with a daughter . . . from about the age of three to twenty-three. You know how rebellious a girl can be when she wants to be free from parental restriction and have her fling. Her parents naturally worry about her staying out late at night and mixing with heaven knows who. However, I was exaggerating when I said three to twenty-three. It definitely wasn't that with Jane. By the time she was four that phase was over.

When Mary and I were at Jane and John's stage there was still a term used for a baby which might surprise some young people. It was called a gift. We looked upon Jane as a gift when she was born and we've continued to look at her like that ever since. She has been to us a cherished gift. Today we entrust that gift to another's care, confident in the soundness of that care.

(GLANCE DOWN) Oh, I nearly forgot to exhaust my list of puns, and there's a bonus one in this. If they have a red-haired child its *nickname* could be 'Coppernob' . . . I think I'm getting into the swing of being a policeman's father-in-law.

Ladies and gentlemen, to wish the happy couple good fortune in their life of taking care of each other, would you please join the toast which it is my privilege to propose, namely the health and happiness of the bride and groom.

Bride's Father No. 6

It doesn't seem long since I stood here and made my first speech as a bride's father. It was a task that I had looked forward to with mixed feelings, and there must be some of the gentlemen here today who will know from experience what I mean.

When you are not a habitual speechmaker it can give you the jitters because you're going to be in the spotlight carrying out a performance that you're not adequately practised in, and you're anxious about remembering most of what you want to say.

On the other hand there is the pleasurable anticipation of having a unique opportunity to express to your family and friends – and that includes newly-acquired family and friends – the feelings that you have as the father of a lovely young lady on her special day.

At the end of that first speech that I made I proposed the traditional toast to the health and happiness of the bride and groom. It worked. Kate and Ron have been as happy as biddies, whatever they are. I don't know what magic potion was slipped into our glasses by some kind fairy when we drank that toast, but our wishes were well and truly fulfilled.

Mary and I were excited when Kate announced that she was getting engaged to Ron, because we had secretly kept our fingers crossed that this would happen. We had seen clearly that he was Mr Right, and we wanted him in the family.

What I'm leading up to is that on this occasion, Jane and John's wedding, I have been less apprehensive about my spell in the spotlight because of my confidence that their partnership is going to follow in the wake of Kate and Ron's. Even if I make a

hash of things and get booed off the stage, it's of little consequence in relation to that.

It is going to be history repeated. I don't mean me getting
booed off the stage, because that didn't happen. I mean the
success of Jane and John's marriage. There is, of course, a little
sadness at the severing of the umbilical cord, but that passes.
Mary and I can rejoice that the second of our lovely daughters has
made a match with her Mr Right, and indeed, as with her sister, in
doing so she has brought more welcome people into the family.

Now, what can we tell John about our Jane now that he's well
and truly hooked and it's too late for him to have any second
thoughts about marrying her? He can't have heard everything
about her – not from us, anyway, because we were on our guard
not to put him off her.

Perhaps we should say nothing so that he can at least have
today in blissful ignorance. He'll find out all in good time.

However, on the theme of the happy state of affairs in our own
family circle it is with an inward sigh of relief that Mary and I
have contemplated our own future. Just to point up what can
happen with the break-up of marriages, there was a couple who
were joined together in some kind of matrimony, holy or otherwise, after both having been married previously.

One day the man was looking through the window into their
back garden and he said to the woman, 'You know my kids?' She
said, 'Yes.' He said, 'And you know your kids?' She said, 'Yes.'
He said, 'Well, they're fighting our kids.'

It only remains for me to propose the toast to Jane and John,
and as you drink imagine that while I've been on my feet that
fairy has been on the wing, whipping round invisibly, dropping
more of that same potion into our glasses.

Ladies and gentlemen, I give you the toast to the health and
happiness of Jane and John.

Bride's Father No. 7

(Whirlwind engagement)

When I became aware that this day was fast approaching and I felt it was time to start organising my speech as the bride's father, I was reminded of what I'd been told about another man in the same situation.

He'd popped into the bedroom to change and he took advantage to spend a moment rehearsing part of his speech in front of the mirror. There he was, spreading his hands and gesticulating, when his wife overheard him and looked in. She said, 'Who are you talking to?' He said, 'I'm rehearsing my speech for Saturday.' She said, 'Well, they won't hear a word you say. They'll be too fascinated seeing you standing there in your underpants.' He said, 'That's a good idea. It's one way of making a memorable speech.'

Well, I don't aspire to make a memorable speech for an occasion like this, even if I could. That's not what we're here for. I only wish to use the opportunity to express to you my feelings – and Mary's – about Jane and John becoming man and wife. We couldn't be more happy.

Jane and John had known each other for only a short time before they became engaged. In many cases when that happens and the couple lose no time in putting wedding arrangements into operation it can be a good thing that churches are booked so far in advance that there's a long delay before the wedding can take place. It gives the couple a cooling-off period during which one of them at least may conclude that getting married is a mistake. (PAUSE, THEN HASTILY, AS AN AFTERTHOUGHT) I don't mean they conclude that getting married at all is a mistake, I mean the couple in question marrying each other.

You might think that Mary and I, of all people, would be the anxious ones, and if it had been any other man except John, then, yes, we should have been ill at ease.

As it happened, John was a person that we were able to know very quickly, just as Jane had found, and the person that Mary and I came to know, we liked very much indeed. We recognised in him the qualities that he had in common with Jane, and it was clear that they were made for each other. They are two of a kind and fate brought them together.

The interesting thing is that their early decision to marry was not the result of being impulsive. Those who know Jane well enough also know of her cautious nature, and the same goes for John. No, they were like two pieces of a jigsaw puzzle that matched each other. I dare say that Shakespeare would have expressed that more poetically, but it should suffice to illustrate the point.

Well, time has passed and our confidence has been justified. The lovebirds have deepened their relationship and it's bedrock firm. (PAUSE, THEN TURN TO JANE AND JOHN) I'm sorry, I shouldn't have used that word. There was no innuendo intended. You've got me flustered now ... or rather I've got myself flustered. Now, where was I? ... I know where I wish I was at the moment. I don't know about a blushing bride. I think you've got a blushing bride's father. My speech might be a memorable one after all – memorable just for one gaffe.

Already I have visions of John in seventy years' time saying to Jane, (SQUEAKY OLD VOICE) 'Do you remember your silly old duffer of a dad at our wedding reception saying something about our bedrock relationship?' ... and five minutes later Jane saying, (VERY HIGH-PITCHED SQUEAKY OLD VOICE) 'No, I don't even remember my silly old duffer of a dad.' ...And John saying, 'I still can't work out how he knew about it.'

Sorry about that. I had better get back to the point of my speech which, after all, is to toast the bride and groom. There is much more that I should like to say, but my time is rationed, so forgive me if I appear to end abruptly.

I will simply ask you now please to stand and join with me in the traditional toast.

Here's to the health and happiness of Jane and John.

Bride's Father No. 8

(Bride already living with groom)
(Relates to 'Extra' speech no. 8, on page 279.)

If ever I encounter an old friend that I haven't spoken to for a year or two, and we're catching up on each other's lives, I'm invariably asked about Jane, with the implied question, 'What's she like?' My short answer is that she's a typical 'modern miss'.

What volumes are spoken in that phrase! . . . Some of you might be thinking, 'What a multitude of sins it covers!' but I'm not going to be tactless enough to say that!

Now, what does it mean? What do I mean by it? Thinking about this has made me realise how long the phrase has been used, to my recollection. I remember it from decades ago, so with changing fashion, a 'modern miss' of today must be different from one of yesteryear. One from forty years ago would appear old-fashioned today.

So to be a full-blooded 'modern miss' at any given time means being right up to date with the latest fashions in dress, behaviour, customs and attitudes. To me, central to it also is a rebellion against convention, and a liberation from restriction. The momentum of this rebellion is still with us.

So, Jane, you know what you are – or were – because you are now no longer a 'miss'. You're a 'modern Mrs'.

Now that you're in your twenties you are relatively (and I emphasise 'relatively') staid. I mean, today's really 'with-it' teenage girl daubs herself with half a pound of make-up, whizzes off to late-night parties just when her parents are going to bed, changes her hairstyle and her boyfriend twice a week and indulges in marathon telephone calls sponsored by her father. Her bedroom walls are covered with huge pictures of weird young men sporting guitars, and her idea of a quiet evening at home is to prance about to pop records played loudly enough to make her granddad rejoice to discover that he's not totally deaf after all. One saving grace is that her skirts at least show that she's wearing knickers.

However, what I'm coming to is that we all, by and large, conform to the outward fashions of our own sex and age group. Notice that I say outward fashions. Basic values are a different thing, and they're what matter.

Practices that are the norm in one society can appear eccentric or outrageous to the members of another. Two different societies can be contemporary, but in different parts of the world, or they can be in the very same location, but in different eras. Just think how shocked our Victorian forebears would be if they saw what we get up to today. Well, what you get up to. I don't know about me.

Anyway, the pace of change has accelerated in recent times, and people in my generation can see wide differences within our own lifetime, and ones which we are bemused by.

Jane and John are in the younger generation, and they followed the now common custom of a trial marriage. With us older folk it can still be a reflex action to raise our eyebrows every time we hear of that happening, but I doubt if you'll see many raised eyebrows amongst the younger generation. Their attitudes have been conditioned differently from ours.

What I want to say is that our instinctive conditioned reactions are not necessarily a guide to what is right and what is wrong – precisely because they are conditioned.

Jane and John are an example of two sensible people who did not lightly (if I may use a telling expression) 'shack-up' together. It was because they believed in the dignity of marriage that they wanted to be sure that a marriage between them, if it were entered into, would be a happy one.

Now I'll tell you something else. John's had an exhaustive trial run as a son-in-law. He's passed the test with flying colours. That's what makes Mary and me so happy, that he and Jane have proved to themselves by experience that they are compatible, as they had hoped, and have progressed to marriage.

We welcome John today as a permanent member of the family. Mary and I were relieved and excited when Jane and John said they knew for sure that all was well between them and they planned to marry. We had kept our fingers crossed, because we had become so fond of John and we looked upon him as a son that we had gained. It would have been a sad day indeed if Jane and John had decided that they were not for each other, and would go their separate ways.

I can't help thinking that I'm recounting a fairy tale, and John's parents had a stake in the issue as well. I feel like saying, 'and the princess married her prince and they all lived happily ever after.'

You know, it's customary for the bride's father to flaunt his wisdom about marriage by publicly passing on advice to the newlyweds. It would be farcical for me to do that. *I've* been asking *John* for advice.

Ladies and gentlemen, would you join me in the toast to our happy pair for their continued health and happiness. Jane and John.

Bride's Father No. 9

(Bride a secretary)
(Relates to Best Man's speech no 8, on page 254.)

Before I embark upon a few well-chosen words about my daughter, I should like to attend to some other points, which might otherwise be neglected. *You* might forgive my omissions, but if I overlook certain courtesies and acknowledgements, I stand to get my ears boxed when I get home.

Firstly, Mary and I extend a very warm welcome to all of you to this very special family celebration. We find great pleasure in formally welcoming John into the family. I say 'formally', because he's already made himself at home with us and to all intents and purposes has long been in the family. If I can court danger for a moment, I may say, John, that now you're actually married to Jane, you're well and truly in it.

Mary and I are also extremely happy in the cementing of ties between John's family and ours.

Now, Jane, you'll probably be more interested than anyone to hear what I say in the next few minutes, because it's about you.

Much of what Jane is and does is paralleled in her occupation as a secretary. In fact, it has been greatly to the advantage of her mum and dad that when she has come home from work, she hasn't been able to stop being a secretary.

It's interesting to reflect on the innumerable and varied qualities that can come into play daily in the course of that occupation. There are all kinds of challenges popping up.

The job title 'secretary' can seem colourless compared with, for example, 'air hostess'. It's a bit like 'housewife'. But a housewife can be a self-seeking female who's married a wealthy man in order to live in luxurious ease or she can be an old woman living in a shoe, with so many children that she doesn't know what to do – apart from attending a family planning clinic.

Yes, a secretary is a common enough occupation, but what makes all the difference is the character and the talents that are brought to it. A busy executive relies on a good secretary, and to be a good secretary, a woman has to be an 'all-rounder', and always 'on the ball.'

She may be engrossed in a task when there's a phone call for the boss from somebody that she, in her wisdom, knows that he wouldn't want to speak to at that particular time. Quick thinking and imagination are called for if, like Jane, she has scruples, and doesn't use the easy way out by telling a blatant lie. She may start with, 'It's a bit tricky for him to take the call at the moment,' and if the caller persists, she may add, again without stating a lie, something like, 'Aren't you getting the earthquake very badly where you are, then?' and call, 'Hold that wall up, somebody, while I'm on the phone!'

Sometimes the boss's lady friend might telephone and that can call for instant ingenuity if his wife's called in at the office and she's nearby. The secretary might say in a stage whisper, 'I can't discuss it now because his wife might overhear. He wants the flowers to be a surprise for her.'

When his wife's gone she informs her boss what's happened and orders a bouquet to be sent to his wife with the message, 'I just couldn't wait till your birthday.'

John, you're going to enjoy the benefit of all this prowess in your marriage. You'll not only have a wife, but a built-in, unpaid secretary who will smooth your path besides sweeping it.

Jane will take care of mundane matters, so your mind will be unfettered and free to fly into higher realms – at least, if the experience of Mary and me is anything to go by. While our dear Jane was with us, we wallowed in the luxury of having a self-appointed servant. We came to depend on her too much. When she left home it took us three days to find the pantry.

A man came to the door wanting money for the milk. We thought it was free. Mary said to me one afternoon, 'It's about time we made the bed.' I said, 'Why?' She said, 'It hasn't been done for a fortnight.'

You'll discover, John, that our loss is your gain.

However, we're not complaining, because we've gained you,

and we can still look forward to Jane popping in as often as possible and making herself at home just as if she still lived there. In other words, paying the milkman, making our bed, and so on.

On that happy note I should like to round off by asking you all to stand, please, to toast Jane and John's health and happiness as man and secretarial wife.

Ladies and gentlemen, Jane and John.

Bride's Father No. 10

(Bride a junior school teacher)
(Relates to Bridegroom's speech no. 10, on page 229)

It seems to me that people enter the teaching profession from two different directions. In one direction lies the academic sphere. There are some people with an absorbing interest in a particular subject, who find it a congenial occupation teaching their speciality to others.

From the other direction come the people whose greater interest is in the young, and in their development. Speaking in general terms, the academic tends towards working with older children, where his academic bent comes into its own, whereas the other type is happy amongst younger ones.

This is, of course, the barest of generalisations. There is a great range between the extremes of these two, and many very academic types make a career of working with the youngest of children.

Jane was a 'natural' for younger children, and this is where she can be bossy if she likes with impunity. She might get kicked now and again by an ill-tempered child, but in the main her size compared with that of her charges serves as an efficient deterrent.

It's gratifying for Mary and myself to know that Jane works amongst the children that she loves. Her constant daily practice in managing little ones will stand her in good stead in her own family future, not that we anticipate her having thirty children all about the same age.

That reminds me of a young lady teacher in a railway carriage who was fairly certain that she recognised the man sitting opposite as the parent of a child in her class. She said to him,

'Excuse me, but aren't you the father of one of my children?' . . .
He said, 'No, but can I put my name down?'

Ambiguities constantly cause misunderstandings in children's minds. A minor example is that of the little boy who was asked in a mental arithmetic session, 'What's nine times nineteen?' He said, 'A hundred and seventy-one.' The teacher said, 'Very good!' The boy said, 'What do you mean – "very good"? It's perfect.'

Then there was the occasion – and this is quite true – when a class was told to draw a picture of the Garden of Eden. One little lad had made a quite authentic depiction, but the teacher was puzzled to see a motor car in it. She didn't want to sound critical, so she simply said, 'I recognise Adam and Eve in the back of the car, but who is it in the front?' He said, 'That's God driving them out.'

Another true anecdote (although a name has been changed to protect the innocent) concerns the little girl with a playmate called Robin. She said to her mummy, 'Me and Robin were lucky. We had "secs" at school again today.' Her mummy said, '*What* did you say?' She said, 'Me and Robin had "secs" again at dinner time.' Her horrified mummy said, 'What do you mean – "sex"?' The little girl said, 'You know – "seconds." If there's any dinner or pudding left over, some of us get a second helping.'

John, you will already have heard from Jane quite a few titbits thrown up in the course of a day amongst the very young. Mary and I used to enjoy an almost daily ration of these, and you can look forward to them as a constant source of amusement. It will compensate for irksome little things that happen when Jane forgets that she's not amongst the children, and you get a clip round the ear for mislaying your pen.

Come what may, John, Mary and I have great pleasure in welcoming you into our family.

As far as any advice goes that I can offer to you both, Jane and John, in your married state, perhaps I should follow up what I've said about Jane forgetting that she's not at school, when she's with you, John. Jane, John's a big boy now. Don't embarrass him in front of guests that you have to dinner by correcting the way he uses his knife and fork.

John, for your part, to keep the harmony play safe and do such things as standing up and saying, 'Good morning, Miss' at the start of each day.

Remember that what pleases one partner can displease the other, and you each have to accept displeasure as well as having pleasure.

For instance, when a couple arrived home one evening, their son said to his mother, 'Grandma rang. Which do you want first, the good news or the bad news?' His mother said, 'The good.' The lad said, 'Gran says yes, she *would* like to come and stay with us again.' The mother said, 'And the bad?' he said, 'But only for two days.'

Then he went out to his dad, who was putting the car away, and said, 'Grandma rang. Which do you want first, the good news or the bad news?' His dad said, 'The bad.' The lad said, 'Gran says yes, she *would* like to come and stay with us again.' His dad said, 'And the good?' He said, 'But only for two days.'

Ladies and gentlemen, I should like to propose a toast to our happy couple for their continuing happiness.

Would you raise your glasses please, and drink to the health and happiness of Jane and John.

23

Other Opening Speeches

Other Opening Speeches No. 1
Bride's grandfather

I never imagined that the pleasure of making a speech at Jane's wedding would fall to me. It wouldn't have happened if my little lad hadn't insisted and persisted and every other 'isted' to get me to do this in place of him, because he was convinced that I could make a better job of than he could. That was his way of saying, 'Neither of us could make a decent speech but I'd rather you be in the hot spot than me.'

He wanted to get out of people saying, 'I didn't think much of Frank's speech, did you?' He'd much prefer them to say, 'Didn't old Syd ramble on with a lot of drivel! It's a pity Frank didn't do the speech instead.'

Now you'll know where the blame lies if you have to listen to rambling drivel for the next few minutes. It'll be Frank's fault.

John, before I go any further, one thing that I'm conscious of is that I referred to this occasion as Jane's wedding. Now, Jane couldn't get married on her own. There has to be somebody else getting married at the same time.

(BACK TO GUESTS) What I want to emphasise to John and all of you good folks is that I'm not speaking here as an oddbod. I'm speaking in place of the bride's father. As such I shall be talking far more about Jane than John. (TO JOHN) Anyway, as you are aware, John, you and I have had very little chance to get to know each other yet. Most of what I know about you is only hearsay. Don't you worry about that though, because I do know the truth about one thing. You can't believe all you hear.

What I do rely on, John, is Jane's evaluation of you. It's true that love is blind, but if you were other than the presentable young man that you appear to anyone, then the love wouldn't have been there in the first place. Jane is too shrewd. She gets it from her grandfather.

(BACK TO GUESTS) This is a proud day for the wife and myself as well as for Jane's mum and dad. It's gratifying for us to see our family flourishing. It was difficult enough for us to believe that we were grandparents – time flies so quickly – and now here we are already seeing the baby girl that made us grandparents herself grown up and married. We are both hale and hearty enough to be able to hope that we shall see a great-grandchild. If it's a little girl, then my dearest wish is that when she gets married, it's her granddad who's made to do a speech.

Having been in the wedded state for most of my long life, I am in a position to offer our newlyweds some timely advice. After the euphoria of the early days of marriage the tendency is for the couple to slip imperceptibly into a negative attitude of taking each other for granted. I read a letter to some newspaper or magazine in which a woman complained about husbands taking this attitude. She pointed out that when a man is welcoming a stranger into the house, he often makes the introduction to his wife with the words, 'This is the wife.'

The writer objected to the use of 'the' before 'wife'. She said it gave away the husband's view of his wife as just another piece of furniture. It was like saying, 'This is the table, this is the settee, this is the television set and this is the wife.' A man wrote back and said that the woman who was complaining had misinterpreted the sense in which the word 'the' was used. He said that what a man meant was 'This is *the* wife' – which I thought was quite clever of him.

But to illustrate why a man should never take his wife for granted, there was a bullying type of husband whose wife was weak and submissive. She suffered in silence, bearing in mind her promise to love, honour and obey and so on 'till death us do part'. And this is exactly what she did – right up to the moment she shot him.

Now, it's a commonplace that there has to be 'give and take' in marriage . . . but how much trouble and misery could be avoided if only this were put into practice in its wider meaning! 'Giving' doesn't simply mean a man saying to himself, 'I suppose I'd better take the old cow a bunch of flowers for once, otherwise she'll start moaning – or mooing.' It goes deeper than that.

However, ladies and gentlemen, I think I'll have to continue my offerings of advice to the newlyweds in private instead of taking up any more of your time.

May I now propose the toast to our two fine young people. Would you please join me in wishing them a happy future. Here's to Jane and John.

Other Opening Speeches No. 2
Bride's uncle

There's something I should like to get straight first of all. Some of you will be wondering why Ken has called upon me to speak before Jane's dad does. The reason is that Jane's dad isn't going to speak . . . I was pausing because I thought there'd be shouts of 'Hooray!'

In fact (and you've got me worried now in case there are boos), I am speaking in his place. (GO TO PUT FINGERS IN EARS, GRIMACING IN ANTICIPATION OF BOOING) Right, now we know where we stand. At least, I know where I'm standing.

Now, the substitution was Frank's own doing. He asked me to stand in for him because I have the gift of the gab, as he elegantly phrases it, and he hasn't.

Initially I declined, on the grounds that an amateur speech from a father was better than a professional speech from an uncle. Modesty compels me to point out that I use the word 'professional' very loosely.

However, Frank dug his heels in. It's what he used to do when we were kids, and by jumbo, does it hurt! The soreness still hasn't worn off!

He confessed that he was scared of messing up the delivery of what he wanted to say, and his appeal to me changed to a threat. He said that if I wouldn't do it, and it was left to him, he'd tell you some of the things that I got up to when we were young that would show me in my true colours. That's why it's me talking to you now, instead of Frank.

So to the substance of his message. There are two women in his life, and lovely they are, but my remarks concern today's star attraction, Jane. Now, John's people mustn't be offended at that description being applied to Jane singly. The bride always is the centre of attraction at any wedding. If John had been wearing the wedding dress, then *he* would have been the centre of attraction.

In John's own eyes, more than anybody else's today, Jane must be the star. Am I right, John?

(BACK TO GUESTS) What her dad wants you to know – and especially Jane herself – is that she has been a star attraction for him all her life, and not merely on special occasions, when she'd been the belle of the ball, but also as Cinderella working in the kitchen. She's been everything to him that a daughter could be. She has been, and always will be, Daddy's little girl.

Jane has been a willing helpmate to her dad, whatever job he was doing, and his heart has been gladdened by the knowledge that she loved his company . . . You know, I think he was too shy to say all this himself.

She delighted in doing things for him, and when there was nothing else that could be done, she'd make him a cup of tea. She'd do that on the slightest pretext. She'd make him tea when he arrived home from work, she'd make him tea if he looked a bit tired, she'd make him tea when he'd backed a slow horse, she'd make him tea when he wanted coffee . . . You see that stomach of his? It isn't beer, it's tea. Out of the racing season, it goes down.

Have I got the message across all right, Frank?

You might attribute Frank's lavish parental praise to natural prejudice, but you'd be wrong. I can vouch for the truth of these words that he's said without moving his lips. I can bear witness to the quality of this father-daughter relationship. What I have conveyed to you from Frank is the sort of thing you would have heard had I been speaking to you as from myself.

There's something else that I know from first hand that Frank failed to mention. Jane's devotion is not confined to him. If Mary had been speaking today, she would be singing Jane's praises from the mother's viewpoint.

If there was an acknowledgement that a bride's father left out of his speech, he'd catch out from her mother. If I overlook one, I stand to catch out from her father as well as her mother, so let me get the acknowledgements made.

Frank and Mary extend their thanks to everyone who has

helped towards the wedding, and there's a very special 'thank you' to me for standing in for Frank.

Finally, on Frank and Mary's behalf, I now propose the toast to the bride and groom.

Other Opening Speeches No. 3

Bride's brother
(father deceased)

It's been a particularly gratifying experience for me to take such an important place in Jane's wedding. I've had to be a bit of a father to her for some time past, but if I never quite felt the part before, I do now. To me, it's as if I were father more than brother. Taking Dad's place in Jane's life in various ways is nothing new to me, but this is a crowning event.

Naturally, there have been times when Jane has erred in her ways, and I have taken it upon myself to try and lay down the law with all the authority that I could muster. I've summoned her to my presence and, pacing up and down with hands clasped behind my back. I've lectured her sternly on the folly of consorting with young men unchaperoned. Jane stood there shaking – with laughter.

Well, it goes without saying that Mum has borne the brunt of our situation since we lost Dad, and it is she who has cared for us. Dad's death drew us all three closer together in mutual comfort and support. That slightly fatherly relationship that I've had with Jane is beginning to make me feel a wrench now that she's breaking away.

John, she's all yours now. If she gives you the happiness that she's given to Mum and me, then you are to be envied. Just remember that if Jane does stay out late with young men, it will be no use remonstrating with her. She won't take it seriously.

It's my pleasure now formally to propose the toast to you and Jane, with Mum's loving wishes and mine for your good fortune.

Ladies and gentlemen, would you please join me in drinking to the future happiness of Jane and John.

Other Opening Speeches No. 4
Bride's grandfather
(father ill)

It's difficult for me to say that it's a pleasure to make this speech. Frank's unfortunate illness has deprived him of his joyful privilege. What a pity! How proud he would have been, escorting Jane to the altar! It's just one of those quirks of fate that we have to accept, but our sympathies are with Frank and Mary and Jane in their disappointment.

It's a case of 'on with the motley'. The last thing Frank wants is for the event to be overshadowed. On behalf of all of us I send our thoughts to him for a speedy recovery. He'll naturally be visualising what's going on here and be with us in spirit. I urge Jane especially to bear this in mind, so that her heart will be lighter about her Dad's physical absence.

In the short time that's been available to me to prepare an address in Frank's place, I've tried to conjecture what he might have said about Jane, and also what he wouldn't say.

Let me explain what I mean by that last bit before you get the wrong idea. When someone is very close to you, it can be a matter of not seeing the wood for the trees. A salient aspect of their character comes to be taken so much for granted that you lose conscious sight of it.

I suspect something about Jane that her dad would have overlooked because, to use a different metaphor, it was too much under his nose.

It's common enough to hear a person described as being of a bright and cheery disposition. Thank goodness that there is a generous scattering of such people, because they cheer us up by the briefest of encounters.

Now, Jane is one of that kind, but something more. She looks on the bright side of things. Not all cheery types do that. They can say, quite cheerfully, 'Things will go on getting worse. The country's going to the dogs. When the world gets warmer, the sea will rise higher than inflation.' They say it laughingly, but they believe it. They look on the black side. Their high spirits can cheer us, but their outlook can slightly depress us, mistaken though we know it is to see only bad in the future.

Every cloud has a silver lining. It's an ill wind that blows nobody any good, or as Shakespeare put it, 'Sweet are the uses of adversity.'

I remember one sunny day in Spring when there was a prolonged shower. There was a job that my brother and I wanted to do in the garden that required the ground to be dry. My brother said, 'Don't worry. The rain's drying up as fast as it's coming down.' I said, 'The trouble is, it's coming down as fast as it's drying up.'

That illustrates the two directly opposite ways of looking at the same thing.

We can, furthermore, be quite simply mistaken in our view of a situation, like the chap who was called up for the army during the war. He said to them, 'It's no good you having me. I have one leg shorter than the other.' They said, 'That's all right. The ground where you're going's uneven.'

I've tried to point out that being a jolly person and looking on the bright side do not have to go hand in hand. A quiet person can still be one who looks on the bright side. But when the two are combined, and combined in such a lovely girl as Jane, what a delight we have!

John, if you've been listening carefully, perhaps you'll have appreciated something more about Jane's worth. You can go round boasting, 'My wife's not only jolly. She looks on the bright side of things.' People will probably look at you and wonder which comedian it is that you're taking off.

Incidentally, John, I'd hate you or your people to get the idea that you're considered of small importance in the scheme of things. I've naturally spoken at length about Jane (well, I think I've only said one thing, but I know I've gone on a lot!) because that's what her father would have been expected to do. I could go on and on about her. In fact, a lot of people do go on about her, but that's another matter.

I know you more by reputation than the pleasure of personal contact, John. Happily, now that you're permanently installed in our family there'll be more scope for that pleasure. There's one warning I must give you, though. You've a high reputation to live up to.

I'd like to encompass everybody in my final words, because somebody's just held up a board saying, 'ONE MINUTE'. You and yours, John, are gladly welcomed into Jane's family, and Frank and Mary want everyone present to be thanked for taking part in this celebration.

I would ask you all now to join me, please, in the toast to the happy couple, Jane and John.

Other Opening Speeches No. 5

Bride's uncle
(father deserted, couple already living together)

I've been looking forward to doing this speech because it does give me the opportunity to put you all in the picture about Jane and John.

As Jane's uncle I've been an intimate observer of the family scene, ever since her father unfortunately took his leave. I'm Jane's maternal uncle. I suppose that's how I'd be described. In other words I'm her mother's brother. However, I don't like the thought of being called a *maternal* uncle. It makes me sound effeminate. You might imagine me bottling the fruit. I feel *p*aternal, not *m*aternal, towards Jane. So if I want to be correct and give the whole truth, I can say that I'm her paternal maternal uncle.

It was when her dad left and I naturally took a sympathetic interest in the welfare of my sister and her daughter, that I grew closer to Jane, trying to do what little I could as something of a non-resident substitute father.

This closer contact gave me a better insight into Jane's character. Much of what I learned, although I didn't realise it at the time, was common to all girls. One thing I found out was that they liked young men.

I would have lent what support I could if only for Mary's sake, even if Jane had been a right young . . . blackguard. I don't know whether girls can be blackguards, but the more female equivalent that came to my mind would not have found favour in a wedding speech. The fact that Jane was far from being a right young whatsit made it a pleasure to me to be involved.

In due course a particular one of those young men came on the scene. I think he's here today. (LOOK ROUND UNTIL EYES REST ON JOHN) Yes, here he is. I thought we couldn't keep him out of Jane's wedding. With some of his predecessors it was a case of 'here today and gone tomorrow', but this one is more like 'here today and here to stay'.

When John had got his feet under the table he began to relieve me of some of my attendance upon Jane and her mother. However, the time came when Jane and John wanted to set up a home together, and as a result this happy event is now taking place. Both Jane's mum and I are very pleased that they are now permanently together in a stable and secure relationship.

Now, what advice can I give you both about marriage? You've experienced the married state for quite a while now, and you don't look any the worse for it, but at present there are only the two of you, and that has a habit of changing ... (GLANCE AT JOHN) I believe John's getting the wind up because he's visualising Jane's mum and me and others all moving in with them.

(TO JOHN) No, what I have in mind is not that, but it is something that will entail you and Jane sharing the task of getting the wind up.

Life involves learning by mistakes. But where possible learn by the mistakes of others. That way you get your lessons free.

Proper communication between husband and wife is important. Remember that managing a large family can impose a strain on your relationship at times. A woman was looking down the back garden once and she said to her husband, 'I'd love some orchids.' He nearly had a fit. He thought she said, 'I'd love some *more* kids.'

Anyway, it's high time that I let you all finish what you were saying to each other when you were stopped in order to listen to me.

I ask you now to drink a toast to the continuing health and happiness of Jane and John.

Other Opening Speeches No. 6
Bride's uncle
(parents divorced and not present, bride fostered by uncle and aunt)

I expect that everyone who has been kind enough to accept an invitation to this happy event is aware of the family situation. My wife and I have had the privilege and joy of being guardians to Jane for many years, my wife being Jane's aunt.

When I escorted Jane up the aisle today it was with great pride and joy. To my wife and me she will always be as a daughter.

The one way that we fell short as parents in the early stages was that we tended to spoil our charge. That was because we were eager to make up to her for having been cheated out of a happy life with her own parents. Looking back, we see that we could have done Jane a great injustice if our treatment of her in that way had succeeded. It is to her credit that she was resistant to being spoiled.

In fact, Jane was more of a positive influence on us. She licked us into shape as parents. She sensed where to draw the line and prevent us from being overindulgent with her. She also had to get the message across that she wasn't the helpless little girl that we were treating her as.

As Jane blossomed into a fully-fledged teenager, she was introducing us to the outside world. This wasn't the world that we lived in. We fondly imagined that we were *au fait* with modern society, but we didn't know the half of it. We began to feel that Jane had adopted us, instead of the other way about, and that she was bringing us up.

Jane, you have kindly intimated to us time and again your

gratitude for taking you on board, as it were. Now Mary and I have the intense pleasure of making it known to all family and friends here that we are endlessly grateful to you for what you have given us in return.

I used the nautical expression 'on board', and when you'd had time to look around you must have thought that our ship was 'Noah's Ark'. It wasn't that there were courting couples of giraffes and whatnot about, but the general atmosphere of being behind the times. I suppose you thought I was Noah. I wonder if that was why, when we were discussing a name for the house, you suggested 'The Ark'.

I think it was the little things that gave us away, like when you were doing a crossword and one of the clues was 'a modern dance' in six letters and I said, 'The veleta'. Then there was the time that a canvasser called, trying to get us to modernise our lighting – and I said we weren't going to squander money like that. We'd stick to gas.

To my wife and me Jane came as a breath of fresh air, and she has continued to blow through our lives as such. When she announced her engagement to John we could only be delighted.

John, you already know the extent of your welcome into such family as Jane possesses. Because my wife and I look on Jane as a daughter, we ask the favour of looking on you as a son.

The bride's father – or his substitute – usually trots out some advice on marriage in his speech, but with your common sense and Jane's, I can't think of anything at this stage that wouldn't be superfluous, so I'll waive the tradition.

It is with the greatest of pleasure, and perhaps tears in my eyes, that I propose the toast to the welfare of our bride and groom.

Would you all rise, please, and drink with me to the future health and happiness of Jane and John.

24

Bridegroom's Speeches

Bridegroom No. 1

First of all I should like to thank Jane's Dad for his kind words. Secondly I should like to get a dig at him for making such a good speech, because I'm having to follow it. Mine will undoubtedly suffer by comparison – and I myself am suffering enough at having to make a speech at all. I think if you asked elderly bachelors why they never married, many would reply that it was through fear of making a speech at the wedding reception.

Be that as it may, you can take it from me that whatever I do say springs from the heart and is not a clutching at platitudes. That's the trouble with platitudes. You may wish to express a feeling simply and sincerely and it comes out as a commonplace, with nothing to indicate the depth of feeling behind it, such as when I first said to Jane, 'I love you'. That's why I've never bothered to say it to her again.

Anyway, actions speak louder than words and I've had time to prove my love to her, otherwise I don't suppose that she would be sitting where she is today – or if she were sitting there, I wouldn't be standing here. There'd be a different lucky man standing in my place.

I should like to thank all of you, on behalf of Jane and myself, simply for being here on our great day. You all look very happy, apart from George there, but he never looks happy even when he is. I think that's the best way that you could have blessed our marriage. It's a wonderful feeling to look round and see our families and friends chatting freely together with such gaiety as though there were something good to celebrate, and I feel a little humbled by it, because it means that you approve of Jane and me being entrusted to each other's care. It's made me think to myself, 'If I let Jane down in the future, I'd be letting all of these special people down,' so you can see how valuable your presence is. Thank you, indeed.

Of course everyone who has been blessed with a happy home life recognises how fortunate he or she has been when they learn of the unhappiness of children in other circumstances, and they feel that they have received a priceless gift from their parents, something which is beyond reciprocation. They are quite right. I know, because I am one of those fortunate ones.

Now that I am married I feel there is a way to reciprocate, at least partly, even though that way is an indirect one, and that is by emulating my parents – well, one of them, because I can be a good father, even if I can't be a good mother. That's where Jane comes in. If I give to our offspring what my parents gave to me, they will surely be gratified to see their example bearing fruit.

During the time that Jane and I were engaged there was an episode when I was struck with anxiety about our future married state. It happened when I entered the lounge at Jane's. She was visibly startled and before she rose to greet me she hurriedly hid a book under the cushion where she was sitting. She looked very flustered, but I pretended not to notice anything unusual. As soon as she'd gone into the kitchen to make some tea, I whipped the cushion aside to see what the book was – and I was shocked . . . It was called 'How to boil an egg'. Can you imagine how I felt!

However, when I confronted Jane with it she assured me that the title was only a light-hearted one, and that egg boiling didn't occupy the book from cover to cover. There was more to it than that. I was greatly relieved to learn that not only could I look forward to a boiled egg from Jane, but bacon to go with it.

Now, Jane and I would like to convey our special thanks to Ken, my best man, for the flair with which he has discharged his duties – but don't think they're finished yet, Ken. May his best man be as good to him when his turn comes, as he has been to me. Without him I might have put the ring on the wrong finger, and found myself married to the vicar.

Jane joins me in thanking her parents heartily for providing this day for us. Thank you indeed, Mr and Mrs Jones.

Finally, I turn my attention gladly to those lovely young ladies, our bridesmaids. They have done us proud and attracted many an admiring glance. It seems a waste that they can't be bridesmaids a lot more often before they're snapped up as brides. Why not start a business – 'Rent a bridesmaid?' Well at least we have had the pleasure of their gracious services and decorative presence.

Ladies and gentlemen, may I ask you to rise and join a toast to our unforgettable bridesmaids.

Bridegroom No. 2

First of all, on behalf of Jane as well as myself, I should like to thank Mr Jones for all the nice wishes for us that he's expressed. It was interesting for me listening to him, because I've learned a lot more about Jane than I ever knew before. It's given me food for thought. If I'm not mistaken there was a bit of gloating going on inside Jane's dad because he and her mum had succeeded in palming off their daughter onto an unsuspecting victim.

However, one has to take the good with the bad, the rough with the smooth, the ups with the downs, the ins with the outs, and so on. From the good and smooth and ups and ins that I know about Jane they'll more than compensate for their opposites.

Fortune smiled on me the day that we met. I had a win on the pools. That reminds me of a conversation that I was in on where a young chap desperate to gain the hand of a certain young lady asked our older, long married acquaintance, 'How did you win your bride?' He said, 'In a raffle.' The lovesick young one was taken back by this outright cynicism and the older man then looked down and said wistfully, 'I wish I'd won the *first* prize. It was one pound fifty.'

I dare say that in time to come I might trot that out about Jane, but something that I am sure of is that there will be no grain of cynicism in it. (TURN TO JANE IN SLIGHT ALARM) I assume your dad was joking in some of the things he said about you! (BACK TO GUESTS) Getting cold feet is something you're supposed to do *before* the wedding ceremony, not after it. My feet have started to feel chilly. I'll imagine Jane handing me my slippers that she's warmed by the fire when I've come in from clearing the snow away ... and taking the dog for a walk ... and doing the shopping ... and doing errands. I think there's another one to add to my 'good and bad' list – taking the warm with the cold.

It's something for a bridegroom to be grateful for that his parents don't have to make a speech. It's bad enough knowing – or rather not knowing – what your best man's going to say to embarrass you. There's always the consolation that people don't believe the best man, because he's supposed to entertain the guests with a tissue of lies. Now that I've said that, I'm afraid Ken will abandon his prepared material and say all nice things about me and you won't believe them.

Before my thoughts stray, let me get my 'thank you's' in, because they're important. Apart from the question mark over his coming speech, I'd like to thank Ken for the way he has carried out his best man offices. He has afforded me, for one, considerable amusement and I thank him heartily ... Well, we know a best man can get confused, because it's not something he does every day, but I mean, when the vicar asked, 'Wilt thou have this man to thy wedded husband ...?' and Ken said, 'Yes,' I thought it was a bit much ... It's a good job it wasn't the first wedding that the vicar had ever conducted, otherwise he might have been thrown off course.

It's natural for a young person starting married life to think back over his or her past and to ask questions. This is a kind of watershed and the mind travels back nostalgically. It's not so much the more adult years when, like myself, you've set yourselves up in a flat, but the earlier part of your life when you were being brought up, as the expression goes.

Now, when I looked at myself in the mirror this morning when I was all set to start off for the church, I thought, 'What a fine, upstanding young chap! Your parents did a good job with you!' That's why I want to congratulate Mum and Dad on the wonderful job that they did, and to thank them for it.

That sounds pathetically inadequate now that I've said it. It's only taken a few seconds. How can a few seconds cover seventeen or eighteen years? Well, if I went on for ten minutes the question would be, 'How can ten minutes cover seventeen or eighteen years?' So let's leave it at that. Perhaps, hopefully, it will say as much as could be said in the brief time at my disposal.

I will simply say to Mum and Dad, 'Thank you for everything.' Only they and I know what is contained in the word 'everything'.

I only hope that as the future unfolds, Jane and I don't have to deal with such an awkward cuss as I was. The saying, 'Like father, like son' sends a chill down my spine.

My next bouquet of thanks goes to Jane's parents. Firstly, I'd like to thank them for having Jane, and secondly for letting me have her. I'm grateful to them for accepting me from the start, when Jane took me into their home and said, 'Look what I've found.'

Now I speak on behalf of Jane also, because we both want to thank you all for being here and for all your good wishes and indeed those exciting-looking gifts that we've only had time to glimpse at. I can't wait till the honeymoon's over so that we can get back and look at them properly.

Jane and I wish to express our very real gratitude to her mum and dad for 'giving' us this day. We thank them for their kindness in being unsparing to make our send-off so memorable.

A special thanks now to some special people today. What would a wedding be like without bridesmaids? Ours might not have been bridesmaids before, but they've conducted themselves with such poise that you wouldn't know it. When I say that they've decorated the church and this room I don't mean they used distemper and a brush.

What better note to end on than a toast to those young ladies, whom Jane and I thank heartily for being the icing on today's cake!

Ladies and gentlemen, would you join in that toast please. The bridesmaids.

Bridegroom No. 3

(He has been a tearaway)

This is a day that I've been looking forward to with great delight – not because of the wedding, but because of this opportunity to get up and say what I think to the whole circle of my family and friends. It is something to relish because I've done it before. I was a best man and I revelled in the prospect of being able to say not so much what I thought, but what I didn't think. The best man can take the mickey out of the groom as much as he likes.

Come to think of it I might have been premature in my anticipation, because the boot could be on the other foot this time. I'm not in the happy position of being able to use somebody as an Aunt Sally, because the bridegroom's speech is constrained to moderate limits in that direction, but for all I know Ken might have a store of coconuts ready to throw at me.

What frustrates me is the order in which speeches are made. If I indulge in derogatory statements about Ken, he has the advantage of denying them and turning the tables on me when he makes his speech. I'm not allowed to make another speech after him, in which I could redress the balance.

Ladies and gentlemen, the best thing, I think, if you don't mind, is if you all put your hands over your ears throughout Ken's speech.

Now, I want to thank Jane's dad for his exposé of my future wife's . . . I mean my present wife's . . . well, my one and only wife's foibles. Some I'd already come across, but others were news to me. She must have been saving them up till we were married. One day I could open a drawer and find it full of foibles.

It's a bit disconcerting, isn't it, when only an hour or two after you've married somebody you start finding out a lot about them that you didn't already know. If I'd overheard Mr Jones rehearsing his speech before the wedding, I might have called it off. It's not so much what he's told us that worries me as what he might have left out. My tearaway days are over.

I'll tell you about my misspent youth by way of thanking my parents for putting up with me. If it weren't for their dedication to the cause of saving me from myself I shouldn't be standing here now as an acceptable husband for Jane. It was their unflagging patience and perseverance that won out in the end and made me pull myself together. What a burden to them I must have been!

My rebelliousness started early in life. Mum and Dad worried when I stopped out so late. Mum would stand on the doorstep calling, 'Johnny, where are you! It's past your bedtime!' Midnight is a bit late for a seven-year-old, isn't it?

From then on it was downhill all the way. When I was sixteen I crept back into the house at one o'clock in the morning and Mum said, 'What time do you call this! You should have been in bed two hours ago!' I said, 'I was.'

Night after night I arrived home the worse for drink and tried to hide it, like when I sat calmly looking at the newspaper until Dad pointed out that it was upside down, so I tried to stand on my head.

There isn't time, thank goodness, to tell you all the gory details. The important point is that Mum and Dad suffered me when they could easily have thrown me out in my late 'teens'. Instead they were determined to reform me, exhausting every form of persuasion and coercion. In the end it paid off. I don't think there's any need for me to labour the point any more.

Those wretched years are water under the bridge. Meeting Jane was timely. She helped me along my road to recovery. Her steadying influence should not be underestimated. She was something new in my life that gave me a sense of purpose and transformed me. From irresponsibility I was led into responsibility. It's not every ne'er-do-well that is lucky enough to have a Jane come into his life and join with him like this. I owe Jane as well as Mum and Dad a deep debt of gratitude.

Well, Ken, it might seem to our guests that I have pre-empted a good deal of what you were going to say about me. Now that I've come clean, I've probably ruined your speech. You were put on the spot really because as best man you're supposed to pile the agony on for the fun of things, and however bad the things were that you said they wouldn't have been far from the truth. You could have been embarrassed by your own speech. Just make up some nice things about me as you go along. Imagine that you're talking about yourself, then it shouldn't be too difficult. (BACK TO GUESTS) That can be taken two ways, can't it?

Now that I've unburdened myself about my disgraceful past I feel the need of a drink, so if you good people don't mind, I'll end my speech, but before I do so let me say that it's great to have you all here together.

I don't think I've yet thanked you from both of us for all your presents – and the good wishes that have come with them. In any case you'll be hearing from us about your gifts individually.

Not least we want to thank Jane's mum and dad for providing this wonderful day for us. It is not only your generosity, Mr and Mrs Jones, for which we are grateful, but the enthusiastic spirit with which you have organised things. Thank you so much.

There are people we wanted to thank for their help in the preparations for today. I apologise for my mental block – I'm sorry I can't just reel their names off, but your services are not undervalued, I can assure you. Jane and I will see you afterwards to thank you again in person.

There is one small group of people that I'm not forgetting to convey our thanks to, probably because their youthful glitter commands my attention. Thank you, dear bridesmaids, for the help that you have been at the service. You get ten out of ten for that, and ten out of ten for your delightful appearance. That's twenty out of ten altogether, and that can't be bad. You can still sit there looking pretty while the rest of us honour you with a toast.

Ladies and gentlemen, will you join me in raising our glasses to the bridesmaids.

Bridegroom No. 4

(Brought up without a father)

Now that I'm leaving my mother's tender care and starting a new home life, I'd like to thank Mum *for* that tender care and for my upbringing.

After we lost Dad life was difficult for Mum with us lads to cope with, but cope with us she did, well and truly! If she wasn't either quelling a squabble or darning a pocket or trying to find school dinner money, she was doing all three at the same time.

Mum had to read the Riot Act to us so often that eventually she knew it off by heart.

If she has any reward, it's in seeing the fine, upstanding sons that we have become. Isn't that right, lads! In fact I'm so fine and upstanding that even such a sought-after young lady as Jane agreed to marry me . . . even if she was blind drunk at the time.

Mum has at last acquired a daughter, and the odds are it won't be the only one. Jane has landed herself with an assortment of brothers that she didn't bargain for, but she's prepared to take the good with the bad . . . I'm the good and they're the bad. (That's another two dozen tin cans tied on the back of the car.)

Mum's happy that I've married one of the 'girl next door' kind. I know a middle-aged couple and the man told me that his was an instance of marrying the girl who actually lived next door . . . He wishes she still did.

As we lads have got a bit older we've taken a share with the chores, because it was a lot for Mum, but life's going to be different for me now because Jane will only have the two of us to look after, so she should manage without any help from me.

I shall lie in bed on a Sunday morning studying the breakfast menu and give Jane my order as soon as she's back from her paper round. This is what's expected of the 'girl next door' type, so Jane should take my expectations as a compliment.

If you want to determine fully what is meant by one description you should think about its opposite, with which you may be more familiar.

What is your image of a young woman the opposite of the 'girl next door' type? You'll surely agree that she's not a home-loving, caring wife, but a self-seeking good-time girl who wants all she can get out of life and neglects her husband, whom she looks upon as somebody to provide for her, the more luxuriously the better.

She's the sort who wouldn't dream of waiting on her husband hand and foot – which I am sure Jane dreams of. She expects to be taken out for a meal on her birthday because she can't be bothered to cook 365 days of the year.

She thinks herself hard done by if she doesn't get a little surprise gift now and then, like a few flowers – as if her husband's got nothing better to do with his money than lash out in wasteful ways like that. He's got to skimp and save to keep taking his turn paying for rounds of drinks every evening, with his friends.

This is how selfish and thoughtless such a person is. Once the ring is on the finger they think they can put their feet up and take their ease, while the poor husband has to do everything from cleaning his own shoes to loading his golf clubs into the car, and fetch and carry for himself every time she's gone gadding off to the dentist's.

Anyway, I really must be brief now or else the plane will go without Jane and me for a start. I, personally, would like to thank Jane's parents for the way they've befriended Mum. I thank them as well for oiling the wheels for me and Jane. I don't mean on the wedding car, I mean for things like going out for a walk in a thunderstorm when I called round to see her.

What we both want to thank them for is providing the wedding itself. Things could not have been nicer. We really are appreciative of what you have done.

Jane and I want to thank everybody for the wonderful array of gifts. We would love to spend more time looking at them, but that will have to wait.

Ken, you must be singled out for a personal 'thank you' from me in the way of help and support as my best man. You've done a lot behind the scenes. I just hope that that bridesmaid doesn't tell her mother.

That brings me to what Jane has asked me to do – to acknowledge how helpful those pretty young bridesmaids have been to her. We both thank you sincerely.

What better way for me to end than by proposing their health and happiness? Bridesmaids, prepare to be toasted. You all look very healthy and happy, but our wish is for that to continue.

So, ladies and gentlemen, I invite you to join me in expressing our appreciation of those young ladies. The bridesmaids!

214

Bridegroom No. 5

More than one person has asked me how I was feeling about making today's speech. I had to confess to something akin to nervousness because it is something new to me. I've never given a bridegroom speech before. In fact I've never given a speech of this nature before. Brief addresses to meetings, yes, and I can't plead inexperience at public speaking up to a point, but this is a different matter.

You're all my family and friends, so why should I approach this performance with a touch of the whatsits? I'll tell you. It's the difference in importance between this and the other usual instances of speaking. You might think it would be the other way about – that addressing a gathering of people outside the circle of family and friends would be more likely to cause jitters than this free-and-easy occasion. No. Even though this is that kind of occasion, there are important things that I want to be sure to say and I'm afraid of overlooking them.

The point is that I've discussed with Jane the acknowledgements that we both want to make, and if I do forget any then not only shall I kick myself afterwards, but Jane might kick me as well. That's the sort of 'oneness' that we already have, you see . . . At least, if I do fall down on the job, I'll get a kick out of it.

Now, Jane, you thought you knew all the 'thank you's that were going into my speech, didn't you? Well, there's one you didn't know about, and that's coming first. I thank you, Jane, for becoming my lovely bride. You can't help being lovely, but you could help becoming my bride. In my preliminary notes I left a

215

pause after that for anybody who wanted to go, 'Oh, isn't that sweet!'

Those who didn't have that reaction probably consider it an odd thing for a groom to say publicly. Surely he could write himself a reminder to say it to his bride in private. But then why do we make acknowledgements publicly when we've already made them in private or intend to do so? It's because the thanking in public (that word doesn't sound right for us lot, but you know what I mean) not only adds weight to it, but by drawing everybody's attention to where thanks are due, it is hoped that the party on the receiving end better appreciates the sincerity of those thanks.

You might wonder why I should be grateful to Jane for marrying me. I suppose it's because I feel that I don't deserve her. (LOOK DOWN AT NOTES AND SAY 'Pause for spontaneous outbursts of protest.') She's been a good influence on me already, and I feel I've become a better person for knowing her. She brings out the best in me. Perhaps if I hadn't become an improvement on what she first found, she wouldn't have married me.

Turning to my mum and dad, they've been kindness itself to me and my brothers and sisters. With such a mixed bunch as we turned out to be, it must have taxed their ingenuity to bring us all up, but they succeeded admirably. Thank you, Mum and Dad, for everything. There was always harmony between yourselves in the home and you worked as a team. That's something I know now with hindsight. It formed the basis for your success in dealing with us individually and keeping relations between us kids on an even keel. If you were to be paid in money for the years that you worked at that, you would be millionaires.

Talking about Jane influencing me for good, it's worth remembering that in marriage one partner often becomes like the other. I can't decide which would be better – Jane ending up bald and with a moustache, or myself flitting about in a dress . . . It would confuse the kids. In fact, if it happened too soon, it's unlikely that there'd be any.

You do hear some frightening tales about married life though, don't you? Some men vow that they wouldn't venture into the dark unknown of matrimony, and warn others of the evils that wait in store for the unwary bridegroom. That reminds me, I haven't yet thanked you, Ken, for being so conscientious as my best man. Thank you also for your advice ever since you heard that I intended to wed. I hope I haven't offended you by not taking it.

(BACK TO GUESTS) Thank you, everyone, from Jane and me, for all your good wishes and gifts. They are both greatly appreciated. I don't mean both the gifts, I mean both the good wishes and the gifts.

Thank you also Mr and Mrs Jones, for the bountiful gift of the wedding itself. Jane and I are deeply grateful.

There's one more party for special mention. They're shining away in their glory like little glow-worms. They are reserved till last because I'm privileged to propose a toast to them after thanking them, as I do, for being our bridesmaids and for conducting themselves so beautifully.

Ladies and gentlemen, I should like to finish now on that note. Would you please stand and join me in the toast to the bridesmaids.

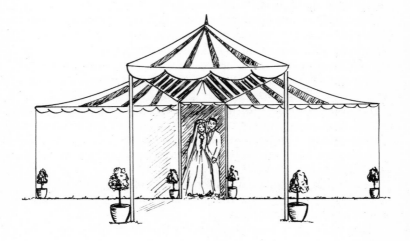

Bridegroom No. 6

(Couple met through dating agency)

There's probably no-one here who isn't aware that Jane and I met through a dating agency. According to a computer we were likely to be suited. That's a laugh for a start. What does a computer understand about people's personalities?

That doesn't invalidate the service that the agencies provide. You see, when any strangers meet for the first time, it's the same situation. They may wish to meet again, but whatever exchange of information has taken place between them, and whatever glimpses they have had of each other's character at first encounter, all this is only superficial.

In a way Jane and I met by chance. We both happened to live in the same area and both happened to register with the same dating agency at around the same time.

When you use those places you can't get anything tailor-made. You have to accept what's going.

A man can go into a tailor's shop for a suit, and if they haven't one that fits him in the material he wants and he likes the look of, then they'll make him one up.

You can't order your ideal partner from a dating agency, but then neither can you from anywhere else. Dating agencies exist to bring two people together who are likely to hit it off. This is what our agency did, and today is the most enjoyable date we've yet had.

I don't know what Ken's got up his sleeve to say on the subject of how Jane and I met. I've talked to him in this vein before, and he might have been going to speak along the same lines. Sorry if I've sabotaged your speech, Ken.

Ken's been a good friend to me, by the way, and after giving the question of his suitability careful thought, I decided against applying to an agency for a best man. It's been interesting for Jane and myself to discover how many things we have in common. It's made us try to recall the details about ourselves that we had given to the agency. But I'm sure that the computer didn't know that neither of us liked streaky bacon.

Of course being different doesn't mean being incompatible. Although actually Jane and I *are* incompatible. I've got the income and Jane is very pattable!

It's the discovery of the differences in temperament and your likes and dislikes that can be fun. Jane and I have found that, and the discoveries that have been made through experiences, rather than by telling each other, have given us some laughs when we've thought about it afterwards. That's one thing that it's important to have in common if you plan to marry – a sense of humour.

Well, enough about us, except that it's we who want to thank you all for your good wishes and gifts. You've given us a wonderful send-off to start our married life. Our respective families have rejoiced in our match and that has enhanced our happiness.

I should like to take this opportunity to thank my mum and dad not only for their interest and encouragement throughout the period of my meeting with and engagement to Jane, but for all that they have done for me and been to me. I am glad that I have been able to give them the happiness of seeing me married to Jane.

We both wish to express our gratitude to Jane's parents for providing the wedding. You have our sincere thanks.

For his special services I thank Ken, my valiant right-hand man, and Jane and I want to thank her little troupe of brides-maids, whose appearance has lent a touch of magic to today's events.

It's a special pleasure for me to propose a toast to them. Ladies and gentlemen, would you please drink with me to the bridesmaids.

Bridegroom No. 7

I'm very glad that I proposed to Jane, because I shouldn't have liked to miss this get-together. I'm delighted to see so many of my friends dressed up to the nines all at the same time. Well done, lads. It's in the best possible cause. I thought some of them might turn up dressed in mourning because it wasn't they who were getting married to Jane.

Well, that's got the compliment to Jane out of the way, so now I can be serious.

But seriously serious, this reminds me of my eighteenth birthday, because the spotlight was on me then, and for no other reason than that I'd survived for eighteen years. I felt then that the celebration in my honour was undeserved because reaching that age had been accomplished with little enough effort on my part. All I'd had to do was keep breathing in between eating and drinking. Yet everybody sang, 'For he's a jolly good fellow!' – even if it was with an embarrassing lack of enthusiasm.

No, if anyone deserved a chorus of recognition on that day, it was my parents. They'd done all the donkey work. They'd brought me up, put me up, put up with me, fed and clothed me, supported me and pointed me in the right direction until I was able to go it alone. Even then they couldn't kick the habit.

Perhaps the tastiest fruit of their labours is for them to see me wed to this lovely girl. (TO JANE) You can say, 'Here, here!' if you want to, Jane.

Many people have told me how lucky I am to be marrying Jane, including Jane. It's puzzling, because they've never explained why. Somebody will lean close to me and say in an earnest and confidential whisper, and with a bit of a nod and a wink, (ACT THIS OUT, LOOKING THIS WAY AND THAT BEFORE SPEAKING) 'You're a very lucky chap to be marrying Jane!'

What does everybody know that I don't? . . . My only theory to date is that it's to do with my dowry, because that's something that hasn't been mentioned yet. Perhaps I'm in for a surprise when it turns out to be a small fortune . . . And there was me worrying that there might not be much left for my dowry after the provision of this wonderful feast that we've just enjoyed. It just shows how wrong you can be.

I do thank Jane's mum and dad from the bottom of my stomach for their generosity. It's been a gourmet's delight, and for me a glutton's delight. I want to thank them also for all the non-edible provisions that they have made. Mr and Mrs Jones have not only provided an entire wedding set-up for me, but they've thrown in their daughter as the bride.

All this means that Mum can now relax in the knowledge that her son will no longer be bringing her his socks to darn. It's been a regular thing. Every six months I've called round home with a suitcase full of socks and holes, the holes usually outnumbering the socks by about three to one. It wasn't so much the amount of darning she objected to as the smell that went with it.

But things are different now. My cases are packed for a honeymoon. One of them's full of hole-ridden socks, and darning them should find Jane something to do for the next two weeks.

It's going to be much more satisfactory for me to have a resident sock-hole mender. It really fills me with gratitude towards Mr and Mrs Jones for passing Jane over to me, and it's incumbent upon me to look after her with loving care for as long as she's useful.

The spotlight is on Jane today, but I want to tell you my own thoughts. It impresses upon me a strong sense of my responsibility – one that I have willingly taken on and solemnly promised to fulfil – a responsibility towards Jane. That's what today's ceremony was all about – the making of vows.

And when today is over, the spotlight will be out and the short-lived ballyhoo will have ended, but the long responsibility will have only begun, and I intend to honour it. So you see, Mr Jones, I don't think you're going to get your dowry back.

This brings me to something else that I almost forgot. It was the idea of you wanting your gifts back that reminded me. Jane and I are so delighted with your gifts and so grateful to you for them.

Ken, to you I owe thanks for your best best-manning. I knew the job would be in capable hands.

Jane and I have been delighted by the sight of our sparkling set of bridesmaids. We'd love to have them with us every day. It's more than a pleasure for me, as my final word, to propose a toast to them.

Would you kindly join me, then, in wishing health and happiness to the bridesmaids.

Bridegroom No. 8

(Bride and groom both divorced)

It might seem a slightly unusual thing for a bridegroom to say at the beginning of his speech that he's thoroughly enjoying the occasion.

Well, I'm thoroughly enjoying this occasion and I'm happy to say so, but why might it sound at all unusual?

I think that for one thing the speech is prepared, not spontaneous and that wouldn't be something written in advance. And the thing is that until the bridegroom's made his speech he's got the thought of it on his mind and he can't properly relax, especially if he's a young man and not accustomed to speechmaking.

I know what I'm talking about because I've been in that position myself, having been married before.

It's different this time, now that I'm older and less inhibited in expressing my thoughts, and my state of mind comes from a deep assurance that the natural harmony between Jane and myself makes our match as good as any. We are both able to sit back and relax and enjoy our day to the full, knowing that, barring misfortune from the outside, we have a happy life before us.

We rejoice because we are both starting a new life. This day is not the consequence of an attitude of, 'Well, we've been friends for a fair while and we seem to get along all right, so we might as well get married.' If I had put that in words to Jane, it wouldn't have sounded a very enthusiastic proposal of marriage, would it? Especially if I'd dropped it out during a lull in the conversation as we were walking through a back alley and I was taking a casual kick at a dustbin in passing.

You don't have to be starry-eyed twenty year-olds to be

excited at the prospect of the life ahead of you. There's such a thing as being young at heart, and the great thing about being young at heart is that you can be like it at any age. It's an attitude to life that you can adopt and cultivate no matter how old you are.

It's a trick of the trade of speechmaking to have a saying up your sleeve to underpin your message. Mine is 'Today is the first day of the rest of your life.'

You can vary 'day' to 'hour' and 'hour' to 'moment', and the truth remains inescapable. The present is always a new beginning, and there's nothing to prevent you from embarking on that new beginning with all the zestful anticipation normally attributed to youth.

This is the spirit in which Jane and I have gone into marriage, and in making plans for our future we have rediscovered the adventure of youth.

I have seen a dull, apathetic outlook in some couples in the springtime of their lives. I can just imagine the aforementioned dustbin serving its turn to provide a moment's stimulus in the life of the young man while he proposed.

Such people are young in their years, but not in their hearts. Jane and I are not young in our years. (Well, I'm not. I don't know Jane's age – she's never told me. In any case, arriving at a woman's age is like converting centigrade to fahrenheit. You take the age she tells you, multiply by nine over five, then add thirty-two.) But we are young in our hearts.

Well now, to come to my friend Ken here, I'd like to thank him profoundly for his services as my best man. What you have seen today of Ken's activities on my behalf – and on Jane's, really – is only part of the story. When you've had a wedding before, like Jane and myself, it's surprising the number of things involved in it that you forget about. Ken has been our salvation by bringing numerous little things to our attention.

I thank you heartily, Ken, from both of us.

Jane and I greatly appreciate everything that has been done for our benefit, and indeed all the kind well-wishing that has come our way from all quarters. It's all been very heartening to us both. It's a grand feeling to know how many sincere friends that one has.

If we'd known that we were going to receive such thoughtful and delightful gifts, we would have got married before now. We are really touched by your generosity, and we thank you very much indeed.

I can't help thinking that with such welcome gifts there's been quite a bit of advice-seeking behind the scenes as to what would please us most, and we have our children to thank for their suggestions.

That reminds me. I shouldn't like to end without a special word of thanks to them for the kind interest that they have shown in the blossoming relationship between Jane and me. Their goodwill has meant a great deal to us. We have rejoiced in knowing that they still feel close family.

Thank you, everyone, for being here. Now please carry on enjoying yourselves.

Bridegroom No. 9

(Marrying late in life)

It's amused me when I've met men considerably my junior but seasoned in marriage and it's come as a distinct surprise to them to learn that an old stager like me had never been married. I suddenly became an object of curiosity. Their reaction was of some incredulity with (dare I say it?) in some cases a hint of envy. (TO JANE) You didn't hear that last bit, did you, Jane?

What they found difficult to take in, so I got the impression, was that I had not been married even *once*, at my stage in life. They'd made real progress. They were already on their second or third wife.

The attitude of these chaps made me feel like a wallflower at a dance. They'd changed partners before I'd even stepped onto the floor.

Why they assumed without question that I was married puzzled me, because I always thought that I went around looking carefree.

That assumption carried through into all kinds of everyday situations. People to whom I was a complete stranger, out of the blue, referred to my 'wife'. Once when I was entitled to a free gift, there was something for me personally and then I was asked my wife's size in tights. I didn't like to say that I hadn't a wife, because that would have changed the subject, and there was another man behind me, waiting to pay for his petrol. Not knowing one tight from another, I acted as if I was trying to call to mind my wife's size, and as I hoped, the usual thing happened – a number was thrown at me interrogatively, and I said, 'Yes'.

I made my escape, wondering if it was the only size they'd got left or if I looked the sort of chap whose wife would fit that size.

This kind of thing happened all the time. If I was buying something at a store and was hesitating because there was a choice, a lady serving would say, 'Your wife would like this one.' . . . Not only was I married, but my wife's tastes were known! These endless references to my wife half convinced me of her existence. It was me, I thought, who was suffering from amnesia.

The one kind of remark that I actually liked was, 'I don't know what your wife will say when you get home!' It was one of the joys of being single. On those occasions I let fly gloatingly with, 'I'm not married!'

It was whenever something was required of me that I could be caught out. A lady canvasser called at the house once and said, 'Good evening. Could I speak to your wife, please?' I had started to go back into the lounge to fetch her when I remembered that I didn't have a wife. If she'd said, 'Is there a lady in the house that I could speak to?' it would have been more sensible.

I wonder what's going to happen now. With a new adjustment to be made, reversing the position, will confusion still reign? If I come home and open the front door, only to have some woman throw her arms round me with protestations of undying love and of how she's missed me while I've been out to get my hair cut, will I phone for the police? Probably not, if I think Jane won't get to hear about it.

Marry in haste, repent at leisure. So goes the old saying. I hope the converse isn't true – 'Marry at leisure, repent in haste'. No, I think we can rule that out. As long as Jane doesn't repent, I won't.

It says a lot for Jane that I'm marrying her. When you think of all the women I've passed over, Jane must have something special. I used to dread leap year. I did think of living in a bunker for twelve months.

However, thank you, Jane, for prizing this old bachelor out of his old – bachelorhood. You have changed my life for me. I shall now be able to go round name-dropping, the name being 'my wife'. I shall get in first with, 'My wife will kill me when I get home!' By the way, Jane, what size are your tights? That's the sort of question I shall have to be prepared for. I shall need to be alert when filling in forms. Where it says, 'marital status', I must remember to put 'married', and answer the questions relevant to that, such as 'size of wife's tights'.

Ken, I want to thank you for looking after me and for controlling today's operations so expertly. You have done well, and I'm grateful.

Now, my wife and I (notice that – not 'Jane and I') have been tickled pink to be the lucky recipients of a delightful assortment of gifts. We really are grateful to you all for your kindness and generosity. We'll be chatting to you about them all in good time. Furthermore, we've been touched by all your good wishes for our future, and we thank you humbly for them.

I think that's all, so please carry on and have a good chinwag. Thank you.

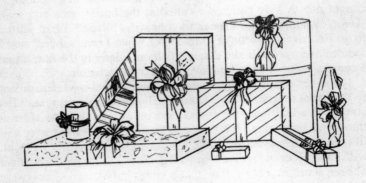

Bridegroom No. 10
(Bride a junior school teacher)
(This speech relates to Bride's Father's speech no. 10, on page 181.)

I should like to thank Mr Jones for his kind warnings to me about what I might expect from Jane in our married life, if her schoolmarm officiousness carries over into our daily relationship.

I've had many years' experience of schoolteaching myself – as a pupil – and hearing that from Jane's dad gave me quite a turn. I think that my fright was a conditioned response, and the conditioning took place in my childhood.

Lost as I have been in my adoration of Jane, it had never clicked with me before now that I had gone as far as proposing marriage to one of a breed that, as a young child, I looked upon as natural adversaries in an endless battle of wits. Is that battle to be recommenced?

There will be one major difference that is a comfort. My physical stature, even though not my mental, now approximates to that of my potential opponent. Jane might be thrown off balance because the ears she's used to clipping are lower down.

You will have gathered that I was not a prize pupil. A prize idiot when it came to certain lessons, perhaps.

Some particular memories of my later days at school come back to me, like the incident with the English teacher who was forever dinning into us that we're all verbose with our first attempt at a piece of writing, and that we should keep reviewing it until we've eliminated every instance of the fault. We should, in a word, prune it.

One day this teacher grabbed me by the scruff of the neck and shot the question at me, 'What do you always do to improve a piece of writing?' I said, 'You prune!' I don't think he understood English, because he ticked me off for that.

A problem at one time was overcrowding. When the girls' cookery and the boys' woodwork were going on in the same cramped room it was chaotic. Somebody made a wooden doughnut.

You hear of some funny incidents with schoolchildren, don't you? A woman shared a railway carriage with a group of girls all working away in complete silence, doing some writing as hard as they could go. She was most impressed. When she got up to leave the train she noticed what they were writing, over and over again – 'I must not behave like a hooligan.'

But what about the violence nowadays towards teachers! Many of them are leaving the profession for safer jobs, like the married couple who've even entered a circus. She's a knife-thrower's assistant and he's a human cannonball.

I expect we could reminisce about school for hours, but the most important thing to me about school concerns Mum and Dad. School was something they worked hard to make me take seriously. I was ushered off to it (and often propelled), in spite of the fact that I was limping with (according to my diagnosis) a broken leg, or that I'd dragged myself bravely from a sick bed to get down to breakfast.

That was one of the many things that my parents did for my ultimate benefit. I thank them for everything they've done for me, right from rocking me to sleep, to making Jane so welcome at home.

Even as I speak, the penny is dropping that part of my feeling of pride in being accepted by Jane as her life partner is the fact of her career. I hadn't realised this before, but it is a kind of achievement for me to have married a young lady such as those whose training and teaching I fought shy of as a small boy.

This achievement is not by a long way my own doing. It can be traced back to the firm hands of Mum and Dad. Indifferent as I may have been (and that applies in both ways – indifferent in ability and in interest in my own attainment), they ensured that I did not evade fulfilling my potential.

If I'd been allowed to go my own sweet way, I would hardly have turned out a suitable match for Jane.

I can foresee a misunderstanding happening repeatedly as

Jane's husband, because it's already happened before. I said to somebody, 'I'm waiting for my fiancée, but she hasn't come home from school yet.' They gave me such a funny look.

It's going to be embarrassing when I am, say, another ten years older and I happen to speak about my wife coming home from school. People will think, 'Fancy a man his age having a child bride!'

Mr and Mrs Jones, Jane and I want to thank you very sincerely for all that you have provided today. You have made it a splendid occasion, and we are deeply grateful.

We also want to thank everyone for all our lovely gifts. We look forward to when we can admire them at our leisure.

Finally we wish to express our appreciation of the service rendered by those young people who have contributed far more to the whole party's enjoyment than I suspect they realise – our wonderful bridesmaids.

(TO BRIDESMAIDS) Yours may have been only a walk-on part, but who could not have been delighted just seeing you walk on!

I will now ask everyone to join me in a toast to your health and happiness.

Ladies and gentlemen, the bridesmaids.

25

Best Man's Speeches

Best Man No. 1

You've all heard about somebody getting cold feet and not turning up at a wedding. Well, you may be surprised to learn that it almost happened with this wedding, and it was only through very determined coercion that it didn't happen. John had me by the scruff of the neck. I know it's an honour to be best man, but to some of us the thought of what can go wrong is frightening. John was asking me, 'Is it... the fear... of losing... the... round ... ring?' He had to keep pausing because he was banging my head on a wall – and he didn't actually say round ring. I substituted 'round' for his word that I won't repeat.

That had been one source of agitation, and some people probably can't understand why the thought of mislaying the ring should inspire such dread in the person responsible for its safe keeping. There are two reasons. It's easy enough, at the appropriate point in the service, for the bridegroom to put the ring on a finger, but the best man has to put his finger on the ring, and it's such a small object and so mobile that it's notoriously elusive. The second reason is the imagined scene if the little scoundrel has somehow given one the slip at the last moment.

Well, I had worked out a contingency plan for that. If I couldn't find the ring I was going to say to the vicar, 'Oh, I know where it is. I had occasion to go into the vestry and while I was there I took it out of my pocket to give it an extra shine. I was distracted by somebody calling my name, and I put it down and walked out without it. I'll just pop and get it.'

Once in the vestry I would make a furtive escape from the church, speed off to another town, stay overnight, and the next day walk into a police station and claim that I was suffering from amnesia. However, that would have caused me so much inconvenience that I thought of a better idea. I persuaded various friends and acquaintances to lend me their rings (ensuring that I accumulated a variety of sizes) and I went into church with the proper ring in one pocket and a dozen assorted fakes in the other. If the proper ring had gone to ground when I went to fish it out, there were enough others to use. I should have passed them to John one at a time till he found one that fitted Jane's finger.

So the ring business was covered and I could dismiss it from my mind. What has given me cold feet is the thought of making a speech. I'd been trying for weeks to put one together and discovered too late that all it amounted to would take up no more than a minute – and that was with stopping half way through to blow my nose. Consequently, I must apologise for not making a speech, apart from saying something about the lad here, which is part of my brief.

What can I say about John that most of you don't already know? Quite a lot, but he wouldn't thank me for it. There is one thing I can tell you. The lads and I are surprised that he ever got near making it to the altar. He used to be so afraid of marriage that he wouldn't go out during leap year. He knew so little about the opposite sex that we gave him tuition. We started outside some toilets where they have the figure of a man on one door and of a woman on the other, and we made him play 'Spot the difference'.

You have the evidence today that our efforts paid off. He's hit the jackpot. It used to be John that was green and now it's us. We're green with envy. We are the hare to his tortoise in the fable.

I must admit that my ordeal of being best man has been endured happily today, because seeing Jane and John united has brought it home to me what a good cause it has been in. It's not only proud parents that are here today, but proud friends. We wish the worthy couple all the happiness that they deserve.

Turning to future brides – and my word, it is a pleasure to turn to them – I have the privilege of speaking on behalf of the bridesmaids. If Jane is today's Cinderella and John is Prince Charming, I'm afraid that the bridesmaids have no chance whatever of being the Ugly Sisters. The compliments that they have received have been so thoroughly deserved, and the thanks for fulfilling their role so delightfully. May I convey to John their appreciation of all his kind words. I'm sure they're only too happy to have been of service and to have given us all such pleasure.

Best Man No. 2

So many young chaps like myself face the prospect of making a speech with trepidation. Believe me, it is understandable. It's all right for folks who're used to it. They've gained confidence.

Now, it worried me sick when I knew that I was in for the ordeal, until I started to find out the sort of thing I was supposed to say. This opened up such a vista of opportunity that my fears were dispelled. What dispelled them was a growing excitement of malicious glee, because I was assured that I could say what I liked about the groom and he had to take it all in good part.

I got carried away with my written preparations and I looked back on an ocean of evil fiction with any semblance of truth lost beyond the horizon. The annoying thought crept in that my picture of John was so black that you kind people wouldn't believe it, so the whole thing has had to be toned down to a dull grey.

But then too many of you already know that John is neither dull nor grey. I think I'll abandon the whole idea of gratifying my sadistic streak and come clean.

John is a colourful character. This might account for my spite. I'm not colourful. But I'll allow myself a few potshots at him. After all, he's the lucky man with this beautiful bride, not me . . . not that he would have wanted me, but that's beside the point.

I knew John at school and he shone, whereas I only flickered. He shone as a personality rather than as an academic achiever. I know he won't mind my saying that because he never tried to conceal his limitations on the academic side. In fact it's a joke to him. It was a joke to the school staff as well.

I remember one of John's school reports that he showed me.

He'd made a name for himself at football and the sports master's comment for that subject was 'Can't put a foot wrong'. The maths teacher had followed this up with 'Can't put a foot right.' He still thinks that a square foot is some kind of physical deformity.

But we all knew that when the time came for us pupils to venture into the working world, John's qualities would carry him through . . . How right we were proved! There was nobody who could empty a dustbin onto a cart like John . . . Of course he had to start somewhere before he got a foot on the right ladder, . . . speaking of which, he made an excellent job of that too. When he cleaned people's windows they praised him for getting in the corners. As he explained to me, it was the training he'd received at school. In the Juniors the teachers were always saying to him, 'Get in the corner!'

He went to the Job Centre to see if they could find him a better job. They asked him what sort. He said, 'I'd like to travel in my work,' so they offered him a job as a bus driver.

One thing about John, he can certainly take a joke. So can Jane, of course. She's taken John. There's a fine spirit between them and they couldn't be better suited. When they made their marriage vows today they were both putting a foot right.

John was well prepared for courtship and marriage. In our school, biology lessons were started at an early age. We boys were given diagrams of girls and we had to colour them in.

Talking of girls reminds me of some special ones that are with us. Well, 'young ladies' is a more fitting term for them. They are the bridesmaids, to whom John has gallantly paid tribute. It's my privilege to acknowledge your kind words, John, on their behalf. By the looks on their faces it was obvious that your compliments went down well with them.

Right then, before I stand down – or sit down – let me round off by saying on behalf of all John's chums as well as myself that we are extremely proud and pleased to see him wed to the lovely Jane, for whom we have such admiration. Don't get me wrong there, I didn't mean we admire her for marrying John.

Jane and John, I echo the wishes of everyone who knows you when I say all happiness to you both in your future together.

Best Man No. 3

(Groom a 'high flier')

This is the first time I've been a best man. Thinking about it set me wondering what the record is for being best man the most number of times. Personally I have no ambition to compete for that record. My satisfaction is in performing the function for my close friend here.

I've enjoyed it all so far. That's probably because I haven't bungled anything yet – at least not so that you'd notice. (You didn't notice, did you?) The vital phase, I'm relieved to say, is successfully completed. I managed to steer John into the right church at the right time and get him married to the right bride – and the 'right' in front of 'bride' is the most meaningful.

Jane, you know the saying, 'Behind every great man there's a woman doing something or other.' This is where you come in. Keep behind John doing whatever it is in the saying. So far you have managed it and everything looks good for the future. It's been lovely weather, ideal for the photographs, and luckily for me, in fact, no serious problem has arisen.

I was told of a ghastly experience that some best man dropped in for. Can you imagine what it must be like having to struggle with somebody heavy to get him into church on time because he's paralytic drunk? And then having to hold him up all through the service? . . . You'd think a vicar would know better than to get into that state before conducting a wedding, wouldn't you?

John, you know you should have been fearing this speech because it's supposed to disclose those things about you that you don't want disclosed. I'm expected to divulge murky things about your past. The reason I've been flannelling along is because there isn't enough murk that I know about. You see, Jane, he's too good to be true. He's applied himself diligently to his studies at university and it's kept him out of mischief.

Since John's been back with his old friends, we've been put to shame by the gaps in our knowledge. Conversation with John has thrown light into some of the dark corners of that ignorance. But even I knew that a man of letters wasn't a postman . . . and that 'arry Stottle wasn't landlord of 'The Ignorant Pig'.

With all that John has in his head, it hasn't made it any bigger, thank goodness. And on the subject of heads, it's true that two of them are better than one. Now, as you see before you, there are two fine heads together. Dare I suggest that in time it will be a matter of three or four heads being better than two? I wonder if your two heads can work that out between them.

Jane and John, the world, as they say, is your oyster, and if you don't like oysters, never mind, because pearls can be gleaned from them. You are already at work on the gleaning and producing pearls of wisdom.

Mentioning pearls reminds me of a small, but very decorative string of them, the sight of which has given us all great pleasure today. I refer to the bridesmaids, whom John has so rightly praised.

It falls to me to thank you, John, on their behalf, for what you said.

I think that's all, so I'll close with the wish that Jane and John have all *their* wishes come true.

Best Man No. 4

(Groom a civil servant)

To put first things first I'd like to say a few words about someone who is playing a key role in today's event – myself. I am very important and my extensive contribution to the running of the proceedings should not be underestimated.

I know that because it's in a letter to me from Auntie Annie – in reply to my request for information on a best man's duties that I sent to her Advice Column.

However, I should like to say from the start something that's nothing to do with that lady's advice. It gives me a warm feeling inside to see my friend John with Jane as his bride.

I don't know whether it was his charm and good looks that worked the oracle, or the more likely agent, that black cat in the neighbourhood that tried to live up to the reputation of bringing good luck.

Not that John is undeserving. Our parents' generation are forever complaining about the disappearance of standards and values in all walks of life, but John has begun his chosen career well by insisting upon a revival of the traditions of the Civil Service. He insists upon observing a proper morning tea break . . . That's one of his two main priorities. The other is the *afternoon* tea break.

He learned his lesson from when he went for his interview. At first he was considered unsuitable because he put his foot right in it. They asked him if he'd like some tea, and he said 'No, thank you.' He hadn't heard about the Civil Service magazine – 'One lump or two?'

Mind you, he favours innovations that allow employees more

latitude, such as flexi-time, where you can work over on one day if you want to leave early the next. He's calculated that if he worked through his tea breaks for the next two years he'd be able to retire when he was 39.

Another Civil Service tradition is doing everything in triplicate. Jane might be happy about the thought of twins, but beyond that could be a different matter. There's an annual concert and John's already booked (NAME OF SINGING TRIO OR 'A SINGING TRIO') as the soloist.

Yes, it's not all work and no play in the Civil Service. Their social side is very active. They have darts and snooker and table tennis, a debating society, amateur theatricals . . . plenty to keep themselves occupied until it's time to go home.

But that triplicate business can be a menace. What about when there's a typing error? It once meant there were three bridges built across a river where there shouldn't even have been one!

However, the Civil Service does have an air of respectability and I've noticed the influence on John. When he stands aside to let a lady pass, he goes through the doffing the hat business (GO THROUGH ACTION OF DOFFING HAT) . . . I don't know why, when he's not wearing a hat . . . It makes him look a silly doffer.

He has started to overdo things rather. You've seen him today in his top hat and tails (OR OTHERWISE 'SMART SUIT'). That's what he wears for gardening.

The lads and I have noticed little changes in his behaviour – like scratching his nose with an umbrella . . . and when we're all walking along the street, he makes us keep twenty paces behind him.

Of course there's really nothing wrong with raising one's own standards. It's unfair to call it pretentiousness. When Jane agreed to marry John, he straight away started scouring the papers for somewhere to live . . . I say papers, but in fact it was a Guide to English Stately Homes.

When John goes on holiday, we shouldn't be critical just because he sends a postcard to the Royal Family . . . any more than we should be derisive because he wanted to be chauffeured when he went on the bumper cars. It's a matter of standards. When he and Jane enter their home for the first time as man and wife, he'll get the butler to carry her over the threshold. The gnomes in his garden won't be plastic . . . They'll be real.

We friends of his from our younger days are not surprised at the promise he's showing in his work because he always had a happy knack of using initiative.

Sometimes things rebounded on him, like the time that we accidentally burned somebody's shed down when we went round clearing people's snow away . . . It was John's idea to take a flame thrower. Then there was the time that he led the way on a hiking holiday in Wales, and we got into trouble for trespassing when we took a short cut – through somebody's cottage.

Well, John, I hope Auntie Annie would be satisfied with this. She did say I was to jest at your expense.

Turning to some other very attractive young people here, apart from yourself, John, I noted your choice of words for the bridesmaids. Auntie Annie called them my charges and said I should speak for them, so please accept their thanks for what you said. They've helped to make your day, but I think you've made theirs.

Thank you.

Best Man No. 5

(Bride and groom very young)

The other night, when I was at John's stag party, looking at the very youthful bridegroom-to-be, I was reminded of another drinking bout that I'd been forced to take part in. One very young chap there was newly engaged. I think that was what we were supposed to be celebrating, but as far as everybody was concerned, it was the drinking that mattered, not the excuse for it.

When the hour was mellow, a chap called Peter said to the engaged one, Ian, (DRUNKEN VOICES FOR BOTH MEN) 'Albert, why are you and Marie getting hitched so young?' Ian said, 'Well, Archie, you know me. Any excuse for a party.' Peter said, 'You mean you decided to get married so that we could have this binge! . . . Good idea!' Ian said, 'No. Not this party. A Diamond Wedding party.'

Jane and John are probably getting married early to make sure of a Diamond Wedding celebration. It must have been that bit in a newspaper that I pointed out to John of a couple getting married in their eighties. They didn't look like making it to the Diamond Wedding.

From time to time we do see a newspaper photograph of a couple enjoying that celebration. Jane and John, I must warn you that you'll look like them when your turn comes. Just imagine yourselves – the baldness, the wizened face, the scruffy beard . . . and that's just Jane.

Do you know the name of the anniversary when you've been married for seventy-five years? No kidding, there is one, and do you know what it is? It's Diamond, just the same as for the sixtieth one. It's because they think if you go on for that long

245

you'll be past any recollection that you had a Diamond Wedding fifteen years before.

Talking of photographs, this is probably the only wedding that John has attended which won't yield a crop of grotesque ones because for once he hasn't brought his camera. If I describe John as an amateur photographer I mean 'amateur' rather than 'photographer'.

I can't help suspecting a fault in the manufacture of the lens in that camera of his. If only that accident could be reproduced, it would reap a fortune for the makers for its comic creations. All you have to do is take a snap of somebody in the ordinary way, and the print shows them with one foot three times as large as the other – and the other's already twice its normal size.

I took his first snap of me back to the shop. I said, 'When we asked for them to be enlarged, we meant the whole picture, not my feet.'

When the subject of my speech cropped up between us and my obligation to discuss him, John said that I could tell the truth, the whole truth and nothing but the truth – as long as I restricted myself to the good things about him. Because a one-minute speech would seem ridiculous, that's why I've had to waffle on so much.

One thing about John is that, whatever he does, he always lands on his feet. I first heard this said by the diving instructor when he went swimming at school. A dancing partner of his said something similar – 'Whatever dance we do, he always lands on my feet.' . . . If she'd seen my feet on that photograph she'd have thanked heaven she wasn't dancing with me!

We can't get away from feet with John, can we? He's even gone into marriage feet first, and if there's one thing above all where he's landed on them, it's this. (TO JANE) Don't you agree, Jane? Just blush and giggle. You don't need to say anything. (BACK TO GUESTS) I wish I'd saved that for the end of my speech. It would have made a good footnote.

To be serious for a minute, thinking about the close devotion of Jane and John, a verse comes back to me – I forget which poet it's by – which expresses that, describing a poignant moment of parting. It would be apt to substitute Jane and John's names in it. (PRETEND TO CONCENTRATE ON RECALLING THE LINES)

Jane stood at the doorstep,
As John walked down the street.

Her heart was full of sorrow,
And her boots were full of feet.

Thank you, John, for brightening up the day for the brides-maids with those teasing flatteries of yours. They don't make speeches, so I have to speak for them. May they be as lucky in love as Jane.

(BACK TO GUESTS) That's me about finished, and I hope I haven't put my foot in it.

I wish our couple every happiness, and hope that it won't be too long before they hear the patter of tiny feet.

Best Man No. 6

(Groom works in a tailor's shop)

I won't speak for too long because John's got to get our suits back to the shop. I think the only reason he started to work at that so-called tailor's was so that he could borrow his wedding outfit.

He's got to get them back because they're booked for later on today. There's a bridegroom and best man somewhere, anxiously biting their nails as they stand at a window in their underclothes watching out for some manifestation of the tailor's fast delivery service.

It is to be hoped that the chain doesn't come off that lad's bike again . . . It's not so much the delay, it's the oil he gets all over his hands putting it back on. If they'd only wrap the suits up as a precaution, it would save a lot of trouble. But then what can you expect of a shop that doesn't even take care not to mix up its orders?

There is one thing to be said for them. They're not humourless. They see the funny side of their mistakes. They keep an album of wedding photographs to display their wares. One of them shows a bridegroom with trouser bottoms six inches above his ankles and a jacket so large that page boys are having to hold up the tails. Fortunately he couldn't see himself in a mirror in the complete rigout, because the hat covered his eyes.

I don't know about outfitters. They're the strangest outfit I've ever known . . . They held a sale and claimed that everything in the shop was reduced. All that week the manager was only four foot tall.

During the sale an assistant's glasses were broken in the crush, but he carried on and took the waist measurement of a man who wanted some trousers. When he tried them on he said, 'These are no good to me! You could get two people inside these!' The assistant had put the measuring tape right round him and another customer at the same time.

A contortionist once went in and described to John a weird and wonderful jacket that he wanted for his act. It was something that an audience wouldn't believe anyone could get into, and he wondered if they could possibly make it. John said, 'That's no problem, sir . . . Just help yourself off the rack.'

The time it takes to get a suit made up from there is unbelievable. They claim that all their made-to-measures are bargains. I ordered one from them that was costing me £240, and I said to John, 'I don't see how it's a bargain.' He said, 'It is. With inflation, by the time you get it, it'll be worth four hundred.'

You can imagine that life isn't dull in John's company. Life is full of surprises and John is full of life, so John is full of surprises. To us pals of his the biggest surprise of all has been Jane. I don't mean Jane herself was a surprise. I mean John dating her was, because previously he had freely indulged a whim for going out with weirdos.

When we first heard about Jane, we imagined, from John's record, that she'd have spikes instead of hair, bags painted under her eyes, graffiti on her forehead, earrings looking like bicycle wheels on lavatory chains, probably wearing an overcoat under a miniskirt, luminous yellow tights, and with a black handbag that she could pop a spare pair of wellingtons in.

For all we know, Jane might have been like this when John first met her. That would explain his initial attraction to her. If that's so, it's a good job she changed, because he couldn't have kept her in chewing gum.

John's never known this, but we held a competition between ourselves to see whose vision of a girl came nearest to the one that he ultimately married. We each wrote out descriptions of what we envisaged and one of us sketched pictures from the descriptions. If you're interested in seeing them, we can show them to anybody who's over sixteen . . . No, I'm only kidding, John. Anybody can see them.

Now, what attracted Jane to John? Could it have been his exploits in the field of salesmanship? After all, that shop is a hotbed of it. At any other tailor's if you buy a suit from them, they persuade you to buy a tie to go with it. At John's place, if you buy a tie, you come out with a suit to match it.

Well, that's all the true stuff. I had intended to do some leg-pulling as well, but I think I've spoken for long enough, so if you'll excuse me I'll finish off.

What better way to do so than on the subject of those young treasures, the bridesmaids? It's my privilege to acknowledge John's thanks to them for their service, and I do that with pleasure.

Jane and John, my last word is to wish you your full share of life's happiness.

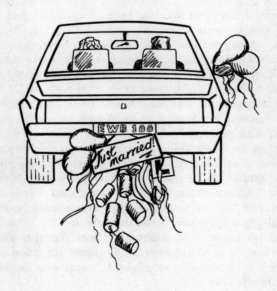

Best Man No. 7

(Rural area, groom originally a 'townie')

When I first knew John, it was when his family came to live here from the town, and as we became friendly I honestly thought, (BROAD LOCAL ACCENT) 'We've got a right one 'ere!'

Being country born and bred myself I couldn't take it in that anybody could be so ignorant of the country.

On his first visit to our farm, John said, 'Ken, do you feed your cows enough? Look, they're eating the grass.' When he saw a flock of sheep he said, 'Why are those animals all following each other like sheep?' he thought a cowpat was something you did to show your approval if they'd given a lot of milk.

He couldn't get used to being wary of this danger and he kept stepping into it. He didn't think the bells of the village church went 'Ding-dong!' but 'Ding-dung!' – because that was how he'd always heard it pronounced in Birmingham. He imagined there was a lookout on the church tower and the bells rang to warn people every time a cow deposited some danger.

When we said that the yew tree was going to come down, he thought somebody was going to demolish a pub.

What puzzled him in his early days was why we other kids in his class were talking to each other in attempts at his dialect, and laughing.

Gradually his manner of speech changed under our influence, and now it's a bit of a hybrid.

Fortunately he stopped asking questions like, 'Are there any yokels about?' and 'Where does the village idiot live?'

When he asked that question of people he was given quite a variety of addresses.

John enlightened me about some of the differences he found. One of them was that where he lived before, the postman used to push seaside cards through the letter box without stopping to read them.

He observed how people here found time to chat to each other during the course of their daily round. In the town potatoes were something you ate. Here they were a topic of conversation. Eggs were things you bought at a grocer's shop. Here they seemed to be everywhere. Even the hens ate so many of them that they came out of their behinds.

Something else that challenged his credulity when he first arrived was the bus service. In the town, when they talked about the bus service, they meant the *service*. Here we meant the *bus*. It niggled him why he never saw two buses passing in opposite directions. It was a long time before he twigged that there was only one bus.

One day he ran for it and just missed it. He asked somebody what time the next one was due and they said, 'On Thursday.'

I suppose our pace of life must have seemed strange to a young boy straight from the hustle and bustle of town. There was a certain old gentleman that John saw setting off on foot up the lane. One of the villagers said, 'That's old Mr So-and-so going to the hairdresser's.' John said, 'But his hair's short.' They said, 'It won't be by the time he gets there.' . . .When his funeral cortege passed, it was the fastest he'd ever been.

John's image of the countryside was limited by all the pastoral pictures that he'd seen. He expected to see all the girls past school age dressed as dairymaids and in the company of cows. He didn't believe that one of them worked in a bank.

Well, John himself is a commuter. To that degree he hasn't been absorbed into what he would call the mud and muck.

Jane, you know what you've done, don't you? You've married one of those townie foreigners.

Incidentally, I think I've spoken long enough and I haven't got round to the fascinating revelations I was going to make about you, Jane. I apologise to everyone for that. It can wait till your Silver Wedding party. You know what we're like round here. Time's no object.

There was a time when John would most likely have imagined bridesmaids at a country wedding tramping manure into the village church. I think that at least he's passed that stage. By what he said about Jane's bridesmaids he implied that they'd taken a fragrance in – and they had.

I'm sure that they would like to make a vocal acknowledgement themselves, but tradition demands that they use a spokesman. That's me. So, John, consider yourself thanked by them.

Jane and John, I wish you every happiness, and John, when you go out of here, just mind where you tread while you're in your wedding shoes.

Best Man No. 8

(Groom of Scottish descent, nervous type)
(Relates to Bride's Father's speech no. 9 on page 178.)

I don't suppose there's anyone here more relieved than I am that this hour has arrived. You wouldn't believe how on edge John has been. Even if we were alone, he'd speak in urgent whispers as if he were scared of being overheard.

It's worried me because if we'd been observed, it would seem as though we were planning a robbery instead of preparing for a wedding. John's even referred to the rehearsals in church as a dummy run.

Can you imagine what it's like when you meet in the street and before he starts talking to you he takes a furtive look round and then speaks out of the side of his mouth?

As soon as he snaps, 'I've got it!' he's got me looking round anxiously and glancing up to check if there are any police spy cameras pointing at us.

Next thing, he fishes something out of his pocket. I can't see what it is because his fist is tightly clenched round it. Then with a sudden movement it's passed to me, and John's looking tense and grim. By pure reflex action I take the mysterious something and slip it into my pocket before anybody notices.

If a policeman had suddenly appeared and asked us the time, I should have bolted. As it was, I'd only taken possession of a small box containing the wedding ring.

Then in the evening came the telephone call, and the anxious question barked at me, 'Is it in a safe place?' I said, 'Yes, it's in Paris.' He said, 'What are you talking about?' I said, 'The Eiffel Tower. What are you talking about?'

No, actually I tried some reassurance. I said, 'I'm not going to tell you where the you-know-what is over the phone in case anybody overhears.' That impressed him. Its location was, in fact, where it would never enter the heads of either the police or a rival gang that it would be. It was hanging on a hook in the kitchen cupboard.

The ring should really have resided in John's keeping until this morning, but he wanted me to safeguard it.

If he himself had been abducted before the wedding, I don't think he'd have worried as long as the ring was safe. In fact, if Jane had been abducted I don't think he'd have worried as long as the ring was safe.

It's become such a fixation with him that it could carry on even now that the ring is on Jane's finger. If she does get kidnapped on the honeymoon I can see John in panic offering a reward for the safe return of the ring. He might reason that as long as he had the ring back, he could always look for another bride to fit it. He could get a new bride for nothing, but he'd have to pay for a new ring.

It's the Scottish blood in him. He had to be persuaded to take Jane somewhere abroad for the honeymoon. He wanted to spend it in this hotel to save travelling expenses. When he finally did enquire at the travel agency about a honeymoon hotel, he asked for a reduction because there'd be two of them sharing a room.

The reason he was smiling so broadly when the photographs were taken outside the church was because it was the first wedding he'd been to where he could walk out without putting any money on the plate.

He's so proud of being Scottish that he's packed something patriotic to hang on the wall of their room when he gets to the hotel. It's a notice that says 'NO TIPPING ALLOWED'.

Jane, your dad has highlighted your virtues as a secretary, so with your cool command over people and situations, things can be left in your capable hands from now on – at least as soon as I've got you both safely into the car for your exit from the scene. What happens to you both on your journey isn't my responsibility – and something will happen, because the car's been 'fixed'. It was part of my duty to organise a joke on the bride and groom for their departure, and I haven't failed in my duty.

Of course, I'm not going to be a spoilsport and say what's been done. You can phone the A.A. if you like, but don't phone me. I just want to relax and enjoy myself and forget all about being a best man.

If there's one thing I'm not joking about, it's my pleasure in speaking for the bridesmaids and thanking you, John, for the good wishes that you have expressed for them.

Jane and John, have a wonderful married life.

Best Man No. 9

(Groom with acting experience)

Keeping company with somebody who's dabbled in amateur dramatics, like John, can be disconcerting. An act can be put on in order to deceive.

Before this makes Jane put her thinking cap on, let me put her mind at ease. Acting usually involves the spoken word, and this is John's weakness. Not that he can't speak convincingly on stage. He can – if he remembers what to say. The memory trouble blights his off-stage acting just the same.

Jane, if John wanted to fool you by saying, 'I've had enough of you! Get out of this house!' he'd go (DO APPROPRIATE ACTION, LOOKING FIERCE, POINTING AT THE DOOR, THEN PUTTING HAND TO HEAD TRYING TO THINK OF THE WORDS. THEN) 'I ... I ... I've ... I've ... I've ... had ...'

If he does remember his lines straight off, he's so surprised that he gets confused with his stage directions, so he'd probably go, 'I've had enough of you! Get out of this house!' (POINT ALL THE WAY ROUND, TRYING TO REMEMBER WHERE THE DOOR IS)

I'll say this for him. He's a trier. When he first started, he dedicated himself to hard work as the path to success. Wherever he went, he could be heard constantly rehearsing, 'To be ... or not to be ...' It was a pity he could never remember any more of that speech.

People overhearing him could be so cruel! They used to call, 'Next!'

Even when we go into a pub he forgets his lines. The gang of us can be at the counter and we have to prompt him – (STAGE WHISPER) 'Four pints, please.'

We had to take precautions for today's ceremony. What you didn't see, but what I can tell you now is that the vicar had an idiot board shoved up his cassock with 'I DO' chalked on one side and 'I WILL' on the other.

(NOW, WITH REFERENCE TO THIS THEME, SOMETHING MAY BE SAID ABOUT THE SPEECH THAT JOHN HAS MADE. IF HE HAS BUNGLED IN ANY WAY, JOKE ABOUT IT. IF NOT, THEN SAY,

'He must have made his speech up as he went along, because if it had been prepared he wouldn't have remembered it.')

But all the world's a stage, and we've seen some interesting action on it in our own little corner of the world today. John must have finally come out with, 'Will you marry me?' after rehearsing it, at least in his mind, as many a young man does if he's the shy type. Knowing John, though, if he did get those four words out in one go, he probably put emphasis where it shouldn't have been, and Jane would be faced with the question, 'Will *you* marry me?' with the implied clause, 'because nobody else will.' Then again it could have been, 'Will you marry *me*?' as though she was thinking about marrying somebody, and John wanted to know if it was him, so that he could announce his engagement.

Anyway, the deed is done. Now, Jane and John, you can look forward to wedded bliss. Absolutely nothing but pure, unadulterated bliss from morning till night for the rest of your married life . . . You can look forward to it, but you won't get it.

Getting married under the delusion that you're setting yourself up for a wonderfully happy, carefree time is like booking a holiday expecting the paradise promised in the travel brochure. It isn't all basking in the sun on soft, golden sands. It's sometimes having to mop up after the rain that's poured through the hole in the hotel roof.

I'm speaking from experience – the experience of millions of happily married people.

I should warn John that in order to achieve a state of affairs as blissful as possible he should mend his bachelor ways. Accustomed as he is to having only himself to answer to in his flat, he will now have to adjust to a new régime.

Someone will notice if he leaves his socks lying about the bedroom floor. It'll be no use him saying, 'They're not mine', as he might have done when he lived with other male sock wearers in the family home.

Of course, that cuts both ways. I don't know whether Jane's

258

untidy, but if John picks up a pair of knickers that are lying about, it's going to pose a difficult question if Jane says, 'They're not mine.'

Other little things John will have to watch are that he transfers his porridge into a dish instead of eating straight out of the saucepan – and washing up after meals instead of putting all the things in together at the end of the week, when he has a bath.

Before finishing, I should like to unburden myself of a feeling of guilt about some exaggeration on my part. In fairness I should tell you that the vicar didn't really have an idiot board under his cassock. It was only a piece of paper.

I'm glad John didn't have to remember that line. He might have said that the vicar had an idiot under his cassock.

Finally, John, on behalf of the bridesmaids, I thank you for your good wishes to them wrapped up in that pretty little speech. Those young ladies can take my word for it that that was no make-believe. As the saying goes, I couldn't agree more with your sentiments.

Best Man No. 10

(Bride a nurse, groom a doctor)

First of all I should like to tell you about a camping holiday I was on with some other lads. We'd gone for a walk and entered a wood. We were deep into it when one of the group tripped and fell, hurting himself badly. We did what we could but he was in considerable pain, and one worried chap said, 'Perhaps we should look for a nurse.' We said, 'Don't be silly! Whoever thought of looking for a nurse in a wood!' . . .But we found a nurse . . . and we found a doctor, too.

And that is how I first met Jane and John . . . because we were later introduced to them by that doctor and nurse.

I've found it interesting listening to John talk about his work. Diagnosis often presents difficulties, and demands astute detective work in medical science to arrive at a conclusion.

John was once faced with a most dirty, unkempt, slovenly young woman, and during his examination of her he stopped and said very thoughtfully, 'How long have you been married?' She said, 'Why?' He said, 'There's some confetti in your ear.'

As a raw recruit to his profession John was naive in some of his diagnoses and suggested treatments.

A fellow student acted as a patient and they started John off with the most trivial complaint they could think of. The 'patient' complained of a tingling sensation in his right leg. John said, 'It's pins and needles. Amputate the leg immediately.' They said, 'Why?' He said, 'To save it spreading to his left leg.'

I remember when I went to the doctor's with an extremely sore throat, and my voice was really hoarse. It had come on badly late in the day, and I was anxious to catch the doctor before surgery closed, so I hurried round. When I arrived the place was deserted, so I knocked on a door, and it was opened by a young receptionist. I said, (STAGE HOARSE WHISPER, SLOWLY) 'Is the doctor in?' She said, (STAGE WHISPER, FURTIVELY) 'No. Come on in.'

I love it when a doctor has an appropriate name, don't you? – like the surgeon, Bertram Frederick Brown. Patients were worried when they saw his name written – 'B.F. BROWN'. A meaningless coincidence like that can, by mere association of ideas, worsen the fear of an already nervous person, irrational though it is.

The surgeon was thoughtful, and in order to dispel people's fear he always made a point of joking about his initials. As a patient was being prepared for an operation he'd go along and laughingly say to them, 'Now forget all about your groundless fear. My initials 'B.F.' don't stand for what you think they do. They stand for Butterfingers.'

Another surgeon had a name that blatantly reminded patients of what was coming to them. It was Cutright. He was eventually persuaded to get it changed . . . John, have you ever heard of Doctor Cutwrong?

Jane, you've probably sensed the embarrassment of some young men with leg injuries at having to take their trousers off in your presence. I was glad to stand with my trousers off in front of a nurse, just to overcome the inhibition. It wasn't for long, because she'd got to get back on duty.

Your dad, Jane, spoke about advice on marriage, and as he and your mother have enjoyed a happy relationship without difficulty let me tell you something about a couple less fortunate.

There was a favourite piece of advice given by a marriage guidance counsellor for restoring the togetherness of the two partners. One couple explained to her that their nerves were so shattered by their unruly gang of children that they constantly bickered at each other. The counsellor trotted out her standard cure for that sort of hostility – 'Think of what it is that you both like doing best, and do it together.' They said, 'We have done. That's how we got all the kids.'

I know it's a bit cruel of me, but before I finish I must throw in a morsel from Jane and John's courtship. In its infancy, before it had become public knowledge, one of the lads happened to see the two of them walking down a lane, holding hands. He told the rest of us about it and when we next met up with Jane we said,

(TEASINGLY) 'We know all about you and John down that lane the other evening!'

Poor Jane was so flustered, and she said, 'I only kissed him!'

One lad said, 'That isn't what we heard!'

(BEND TO LOOK AT NOTES. DURING THE FOLLOWING, LOOSEN UP PHYSICALLY, LOOKING AROUND AND BENDING FORWARD TO MAKE A COMING GLANCE AT YOUR NOTES APPEAR NATURAL)

Ladies and gentlemen, I see that I've come to the final item in my notes, and my closing words are to be an acknowledgement of John's appreciation of the barmaids. (IGNORE ANY REACTION TO THIS).

As much as I agree with his assessment of their appeal, in my opinion this was quite the wrong day to make such saucy and suggestive comments to them. (BEND FORWARD, EYES HAPPEN TO LIGHT ON NOTES AGAIN, SOME HESITATION, A CLOSER LOOK TAKEN, THEN ABJECTLY) Ladies and gentlemen, I do apologise. I'd got here 'B APOSTROPHE MAIDS' – 'B'MAIDS' – and of course it stands for 'BRIDESMAIDS', not 'BARMAIDS'. I'm so sorry. (TO JOHN) I'm sorry about that, John.

Dear bridesmaids, I agree with John about you also, and John, on their behalf, I thank you for your nice remarks and your good wishes.

Now, what I've said apropos the bridesmaids couldn't be more sincere, unlike some of the fibs I've told.

Jane and John, thank you for being such good sports and listening to my shocking slander.

The best of luck to a fine medical team!

26

'Extra' Speeches

'Extra' No. 1

Lady friend of family
(from a feminist viewpoint)

I think it fitting that a few things should be said on this occasion from the female viewpoint. I'm not disparaging the comments made by the gentlemen in their speeches. Far from it, because they have been most complimentary to our sex and they've made some flattering observations. I think you ladies will agree that we could listen to that all day. No, it's merely that men do the speechifying at weddings and ladies rarely get a look in – or a word in. It's one more example of men being given priority over women. Even with my humble self being invited to participate, it's still three men to one woman.

Let's hope it's only a matter of time before we ladies break even with the men, and the bride and chief bridesmaid make speeches. Can you imagine a bride standing there in her wedding dress, declaring that she'll still have her night out with the boys every Wednesday and play football on Sundays, and the chief bridesmaid saying how pretty the bridegroom looks? At least they'll have the opportunity to say what they like to a captive audience.

Unfortunately my wedding service was marred by a series of hiccups. They came from Stan, who hadn't recovered from his stag party . . . You could tell he was still seeing double. When the vicar said, 'Do you take this woman?' he said, 'Which woman?' The only way the vicar could get him to say 'I will' was to ask him if he'd have another drink. When I was asked if I would take him for better or worse, I thought well, it can't get much worse . . . When he signed the register in the vestry it looked as though a bow-legged spider had trodden in some ink and then done the Twist.

Anyway, the point I want to make is the same sort of thing as the unfairness of the male monopoly of the speechmaking. Did you ever hear of a bride staggering up the aisle singing, 'I've got a luvverly bunch of coconuts,' because she hasn't sobered up from her hen party? It's all right for men to behave irresponsibly though, isn't it! Any disgraceful spectacle a man makes of himself is treated by other men as a joke.

Well, I've had my little say, and now on the lighter side I can tell you that in spite of everything, the years that have passed since that memorable day that I've just told you about, have been as happy as I could have wished. The toast to Stan and myself has been fulfilled, and I only hope that the good wishes expressed by all of us for Jane and John's future will materialise just the same. I can't say fairer than that.

It's over to you now, Jane and John, to make your married life a happy one. Having the pleasure of knowing you both well, I know in my heart that you will do this. May God's blessing be with you all the way.

'Extra' No. 2

Bride's sister

It's not often that a sister of the bride is given some time to say her piece at the reception. The truth is that I was nudged into it – well, coerced into it really. The reason given was that Jane and I have always been very close. Mind you, I think it was a shaky excuse for getting me on my hind legs, or any other legs, to impose myself on all of you. I suspect that it was done primarily so I wouldn't feel left out and I do appreciate that.

Anyway, as to our Jane, I can tell you that she's always been the active little extrovert that she is now. Some people who have been at the receiving end of her activities would have used different phraseology from mine. I'm thinking of her younger days. In fact, the farther back we go, the worse it gets.

I had the misfortune to be Jane's elder sister. It doesn't take much imagination to know what that can mean. Looking back, I think that people would have described Jane as a mischievous little tomboy. I was supposed to look after her, but while she was around I needed somebody to look after me. There was never a dull moment, and that can cover a multitude of sins.

She played tricks on me that a little boy's supposed to play on his elder sister. I dreaded her answering the 'phone to my boyfriend when I wasn't in. She'd tell him that I'd gone out with another man, if Dad had happened to give me a lift somewhere in the car.

Later on in life you could tell how close we were getting. We even used the same make-up – mine. In a family clothes are usually handed down. Mine weren't. They were taken. (TO JANE) Do you remember all this, Jane?

It's a funny thing that you can assume that a person has the same image of themselves as a child that someone else in the house has of them. I wonder if Jane thinks I'm painting a false picture of her. I'll balance things up by disclosing the credit side.

I was immature in my sister's earlier years, and failed to see that what I thought was naughtiness was, in fact, merely devilment. It takes all sorts to make a world. (That's a telling statement to make in someone's defence, isn't it?)

Without the Janes, the world would be a duller place – and indeed a poorer place in many respects. Jane's energies have already done more good in the world than most people achieve in a lifetime. She may have taken delight in mischievous tricks in her childhood, but by the same token she takes delight in springing pleasant surprises on people.

From dropping me in it with earlier boyfriends, she's cleverly smoothed things over with later ones, especially with the one I married, and that's probably news to him.

I spoke of the world being a poorer place without its Janes, and my own particular world would have been poorer without this particular Jane. We were close in the past, we remained close when I married, and we'll still be close now that she's married.

'Extra' No. 3

Bride

It's nice to have this opportunity to speak to everybody at once. I wasn't really prepared for it. It was Ken's bright idea. He sprung it on me only a few days ago, when I'd got enough to think about without giving my mind to a speech.

I gave him a flat refusal at first because of the short notice. Mind you, I gave John a flat refusal when he first proposed to me, and yet here I am.

It was afterwards that I began to think that if I only spoke briefly it would be an opportunity to thank all of you for the congratulations and good wishes for John and myself. Then there's all the help that I've had one way or another in preparing for the big day. There are too many names to name.

Those who haven't been closely involved in the run-up have helped with moral support. I never knew what a difference it would make getting married with everybody's blessing. It's made it so much happier, and I do thank you for that.

John has thanked his parents for putting up with him for twenty years or so. (TO JOHN) How old are you, by the way, John?

He's also kindly acknowledged what my mum and dad have done, and I'd like to second that.

I couldn't do justice to thanking my parents for a lifetime of care and love in the short time at my disposal. Suffice it to say that whatever I've done, they've stuck by me through thick and thin, especially when I went on a diet.

I want to thank John's mum and dad for bringing him into the world and giving me something that I can get my teeth into . . . I don't mean love bites. He doesn't quite know what he's let himself in for yet.

Perhaps I could single out somebody (or somebodies) for my own praise, because they are very young people and they've done a special service. You'll know who I mean – and they do, they're beaming away already – my darling bridesmaids.

I think that's about all, unless I can publicly thank John for asking me to marry him for the thirteenth time.

Well, marriage shouldn't be rushed into, should it? It's my opinion that a couple need at least three weeks to get to know each other. I think I knew John well enough after a fortnight, but I was afraid that he didn't really know me, so it was for his own protection that I declined the first twelve times. By the thirteenth time we both knew something more about each other. I knew how persistent he could be and he knew how obstinate I could be.

Well, thank you all again for everything. John's already given you our thanks for your generous gifts. They really have added to our excitement.

Thank you for listening, and now I'll let you carry on enjoying yourselves.

'Extra' No. 4

Son of bride
(Bride's second marriage)

Sue and I have been getting some reactions of surprise and disbelief when we've had occasion to say to people insufficiently acquainted with us, 'My Mum's getting married.'

I suppose it does sound odd coming out just like that. People almost stand back and stare as though they're trying to re-judge our ages, as if their first impression was wildly wrong and they were twenty years out. You could almost see the unspoken thought, such as 'She's left it a bit late, hasn't she?' What we should have said was, 'My Mum's remarrying.'

You see, our mum and dad had lived in a different era – one of order instead of disorder – and they were among those parents who succeeded in keeping that ideal alive for their children. We're conditioned to thinking in terms of the orderliness of family life, that's why we've trotted out that statement in all innocence, without thought of its immediate implication in most people's minds.

It was a devastating blow when we lost Dad, but time has done its healing work even though there has remained a gap in the family. There are Dad's brothers and sisters amongst us, here to celebrate Mum's union with a new partner, Les, so I'm sure that Les won't feel any discomfort if I pay homage to Dad, and let them know that we do not forget him.

I spoke of a gap in the family, and if I say that the family is now rounded out again, it isn't a reference to Les's shape.

Les is one of Mum's generation and he shares her outlook. I suppose this is what brings middle-aged people together. If Les hadn't been like this, I think that Sue and I would have regarded him as a stranger in the camp, as we are both still living with Mum.

There is more than mere rapport between us and Les. There is an understanding and mateyness that promises well for a happy household.

Of course, if he does try to come the heavy-handed father, it will be a different matter. We've made secret plans for if he sends us to bed early or stops our pocket money.

There will be some changes in the division of labour now that Mum's taken on a new hand. As the new man of the house, it will fall to him, for example, to dig the garden and take Mum shopping in the car, as a dutiful husband should. Notice that I did say 'for example.'

Come what may, I hereby wish Mum and Les a very happy future together.

'Extra' No. 5

Groom's godmother

Some of you may not know why I've been singled out to chip in on the speechmaking. It's because I'm John's godmother. Not his fairy godmother, I'm five stone too heavy for that.

As his godmother it's been my duty to encourage him to attend church. Today I am proud to say that I finally made it.

I'll tell you one thing. It's refreshing to attend a good, old-fashioned church wedding where the couple are people you belong with. Jane and John have made a good start.

There's too much cynicism around these days. Mind you, there always has been about marriage and the cynics are usually men. I tried to cheer up a fellow who was disillusioned after his marriage. I said, 'Look, you've got to expect some bad times as well as all the good. Clouds can come over your married life, but all clouds pass on.'

He looked even more despondent, so I said, 'What's the matter?' He said, 'My mother-in-law shows no sign of passing on.'

Then there was the conversation between two businessmen who'd just met. One invited the other to a good night out that he was planning for his pals. A miserable look came over the other's face and he said, 'I can't come. All that week I shall be down at Brighton, shacked up with my secretary.' The first chap said, 'Well, . . . why are you looking so depressed about that?' He said, 'I've been married to her for forty years.'

That reminds me of a cartoon where a very stout, formidable-looking woman had entered her husband's office, crept up behind him and placed her hands over his eyes. The little chap was grinning and giggling away and saying, 'Not now, darling, I'm expecting the wife any minute.'

Nowadays a good many young women are rebelling against the idea of being married. They want to pursue careers instead of trying to find change for the kids' dinner money.

Happy are they who can combine career and marriage . . . Wouldn't you be happy if you'd performed a miracle? Where the couple have young children it can seem like one. It's a matter of skilful planning.

Jane is continuing with her career, but she hopes for welcome interruptions to it.

May she have the best of both worlds, and I can look forward to seeing John in church again for a christening. This time, not his own.

'Extra' No. 6

Bride's mother

As I have the wisdom that comes from experience twenty-five years after my wedding, I'd like to pass a few tips on to Jane. It will give me a chance to carry on about men in general and Frank in particular.

Jane dear, husbands think they're the superior ones, on whom wives depend for their security and protection. This is a myth that originates in the image of a Stone Age man wielding a club to clout dangerous animals at the mouth of the family cave. The only resemblance that your dad has borne to such a specimen is when he's gone for a time without shaving or getting his hair cut, and his club is a place where he spends too much time drinking with his cronies.

If you stop and think about it, which sex is better at survival? If a man's away from home for a week or two the wife can get by with the man's jobs, but you look at the mess a man gets into when his wife goes into hospital for a spell.

He can be hopeless at taking the woman's place, as witness what our neighbour told me about your dad when I was away having you. He had no idea how to peep through curtains without being seen. She called in for a friendly chat over a cup of tea, but he couldn't enter into the spirit of it. He hadn't a bad word to say about anybody.

(TO GUESTS) Apparently he overreached himself with his efforts at cooking. Our neighbour spotted something in the kitchen that she thought was a clever piece of work. She said, 'Did you make that yellow model of a skyscraper?' he said, 'Something went wrong. That was supposed to be a pancake.'

I don't know whether it was plain ignorance or whether he was just being sarcastic about me, but he said he didn't think the vacuum cleaner worked unless you had haircurlers in.

Really, I think if he were a bride, he'd get to the church on time.

Men are good at their own things, of course, like forgetting their wife's birthday and saying the wrong thing in public. When Frank forgot my last birthday and I was telling a friend about it, he said very timidly, 'No, I didn't forget, dear. When you were fifty you said you weren't having them any more.'

I wouldn't have minded so much, but I was only thirty-six . . . or round about that. It was only one figure out. I was forty-six.

This isn't the first time that I've warned Jane about what can lie ahead after the wedding. I've drummed things into her, but John, my dear, in spite of all, she's cheerfully gone ahead and married you. That means that you must be something special.

She's a lucky girl, John, and you're a lucky lad. May luck remain with you both when Jane's no longer a girl and you're no longer a lad.

'Extra' no. 7

Son of divorced or widowed groom

First of all I should like to welcome Brenda into the family. I hope that she finds us as amenable as we find her. We've got along well so far, but when the honeymoon's over and unfortunately she gets to know us better, well . . . let's just hope that she can tolerate us.

The word 'amenable' applied to Brenda, I'm afraid I used thoughtlessly, because she is much more than that. It's how she's going to find us lot that I'm worried about.

You see, Brenda, if you were coming to the house during the engagement, Dad would make us hide all the empty beer cans and tidy up. Then he'd give us a clout round the ear and say, 'And just behave yourselves when Brenda comes!'

The instant the bell rang Dad would say, 'She's 'ere! Get yer feet off the table!' and he'd be at the door like a shot. Then he'd reappear in a state of anti-climax mumbling irritably, 'How many more times do they need telling! We don't *want* double glazing!'

However, when Dad went to the door and we heard, (USE APPROPRIATE VOICE) 'Come in, dear,' we knew that either Dad had had a sudden change of mind and the latest double glazing salesman was in luck, or it was you.

As it happened, each time it was you. Dad would be going on, 'You must be very cold,' or 'You must be very hot,' or 'You must be very wet,' or 'You must be very dry,' . . . It was like getting a weather report. Anyway you were very welcome.

Then we had to watch our 'p's' and 'q's' – or, more to the point, our 'b's' and 'c's'. Thankfully we managed to curb our language, in spite of the force of habit.

After Dad had first met you, we got wind of something, and as the eldest son, it fell to me to assert authority. I would say to Dad, before he went out in the evening, 'Now, I'm not prying. You're old enough to live your own life and have your fling, but just make sure you're back home by nine o'clock.'

But you know how difficult parents can be today. He came home in his own sweet time. I used to say to him, 'My father wouldn't have allowed me to stop out at all hours. I was brought up strictly.'

Brenda, he's your responsibility now. You will have to try and keep a check on him. However, with all Dad's anxiety to make a good impression on you, well, it's a measure of his esteem for you, isn't it? And your magnetic charm will hold him.

We, his family, are over the moon that Dad has won you, and we wish you both the very best of happiness.

'Extra' No. 8

Middle-aged male friend or relative
(Relates to Bride's Father speech no. 8, on page 175.)

Frank has had something to say about changing attitudes, and how right he is! I know of a girl whose mother was shocked when she moved in with her boyfriend. She said to the girl, 'If your great-great-great-grandmother were alive, I don't know what she'd say!' The girl replied, 'Probably – "Look at me. I'm a hundred and thirty and I'm not dead yet!"' '

That's an attitude prevalent among young people today.

Now, I know that Jane and John have already had a few years' experience of the marriage situation, but couples long married can run into trouble with each other, as we all know. Separations and divorces happen at almost any age. I say 'almost' because you don't often hear of a pair in their eighties getting divorced. That's probably because they can't afford it out of their pension. On the other hand they may take the line, 'We've put up with each other for all this time, it's hardly worth splitting up now.'

So I make no apology for offering our happy couple some secondhand advice.

A basic cause of marriage breakdown is that as the newlyweds become oldyweds, the romance that attached them together fades. In their earliest days a young couple may live under a spell which makes them kindly disposed to one another, come what may. They fall over themselves to be tolerant. But when the spell goes, that goes. I'm telling Jane and John this because, whether they know it or not, they're still in the enchanted land, and it's as well for them to be prepared for when they come out of it.

The secret is to maintain tolerance.

I recall a sketch on the stage where an extremely agitated young man was waiting outside a cinema for his fiancée, who was very late. When she did arrive, he flung his arms round her with a sigh of relief and poured out his fears of what might have happened to her.

The second part of the sketch showed the same situation thirty years later. You can imagine how their love had mellowed into something rich and tender. When the woman turned up late, the man stepped forward, took her hand in his, twisted her arm up her back and said, (FIERCELY) 'Where've yer bin?!'

At present John probably sits gazing at Jane across the breakfast table, lost in admiration and blissfully unconscious of his teeth fighting a losing battle with some bread that by a miracle has been transformed into charcoal. Time could change that to, (FIERCELY) 'We've been married for what seems ninety years and you still burn the toast!'

So, my young friends, discipline yourselves to be tolerant, and whenever you clash, don't get your backs up at each other, but talk things over. Some neighbours of mine do that regularly. I can hear them from three doors away.

Jane and John, it feels good to me to have this opportunity to wish you both, with family and friends all listening, every bit of luck that you deserve as truly man and wife.

'Extra' No. 9

Older male friend of groom

I've known John since before he started going out with girls. He used to go about in a pram. If he encountered a little girl he used to gurgle at her. What he gurgled, when translated, was 'Does your mother know you're out?'

It's no secret that Jane is the last in a very long line of the opposite sex that have engaged John's attention . . . well, it might have been a secret from Jane, but it isn't now.

Eventually an influential little fellow took a hand in John's life. His name is Cupid, and he stalks the realms of bachelorhood with safety because he's invisible – and so are his arrows. You can't see them coming, otherwise you could duck.

This happened to John, but fortunately it was Jane who was on the scene. Cupid aimed an arrow at John's heart and scored a bull's-eye. His shots are not always good because he fires balancing on one leg. This can have the opposite effect of what was intended. Even if a young man is struck, he might not get a pain in the heart over a girl, but instead find her a pain in the something else. It's no wonder he's sometimes shown blindfolded.

It's a pity that Cupid's invisible, because from what I've seen of his pictures we could have him arrested for streaking.

At least he's put a stop to John's little gallop. John should only get one Valentine card next time, not dozens. If he does get more than one, there's still only one that he'll be able to display. And there's only one that he'll buy. In the past he's had them at cut price for buying in bulk.

John's practice of spreading his net wide caused him some

problems. Sometimes when he got home his mum or dad would say, 'Oh, by the way, your girlfriend phoned.' He'd say, 'Did she give her name?'

You should have seen his address book with all the girls' telephone numbers in . . . or perhaps you shouldn't if you understand hieroglyphics. It's the first address book I've ever known that needed an 'X' certificate.

There was an episode when John resorted to deceit. Some of his friends were dying to know what a graphologist would see in his handwriting about his flirtatious nature. They kidded John to join with them in submitting samples. It puzzled them why he agreed, until they saw the graphologist's report on him – 'This person is a lecherous young man who thinks he can disguise his handwriting.'

When he was only a little chap he was trying to sort out in his mind how many girls had succumbed to his charms. He was pulling the legs off a centipede and going, (FROWN THOUGHT-FULLY AND ACT THIS OUT, PUTTING DOWN ON ONE SIDE AND THEN THE OTHER) 'She loves me . . . she loves me not . . . she loves me . . . she loves me not . . .'

John, people say that marriage brings its complications. It can't bring you any more complications than you had before you settled on Jane.

My wish is quite uncomplicated. It's simply for the best of happiness for you both.

'Extra' No. 10

Bride
(Divorced, remarrying after a long time)

As you know, I've been married before, but my first wedding reception was in the days before female emancipation and I wasn't invited to speak. Even chaining myself to some railings didn't do the trick. The irony of it was that I only wanted to point out that I admired men so much that I was marrying one of them.

There's a saying that we all know well enough – 'Only a fool makes the same mistake twice.' I'm not making the same mistake twice, or even a different mistake, in marrying John. This couldn't be the same as my first mistake (and it was a mistake) because my fault was in marrying before I was ready for marriage.

I was so shaken by my own blunder that it frightened me off a future union for longer than some young people here have been around. You could say that my second mistake was in not getting married for all that length of time.

Although I say it myself, I was not without suitors throughout my long 'I want to be alone' period. One of them's here today, and that's John.

So what brought that era to a close? Basically it was the gentleman that I've just mentioned. Unlike the others, he wouldn't go away when he was told to. I think that was because I didn't tell him as determinedly as I had told the others. It wasn't because I was becoming exhausted, fending off an endless succession of ardent admirers, but because the phase had run its course. My defences were down.

There were three parties whose concerted efforts finally broke through the barrier. One, of course, was John himself, because, let's face it, I wouldn't marry just anybody simply because I was no longer afraid to marry. That would have been foolhardy.

The second party is plural. Some of my friends had dropped subtle hints, such as, 'Why don't you get married again?' – after John had come into my life. I've given it away there, haven't I, saying 'into my life'. It's a telling expression.

The third party was Old Father Time. He was nudging things along, saying, 'Enough is enough.'

Well, thank you, John, for coming along just when the time was ripe. You weren't just anybody at the right time, you were the right man at the right time.

Thank you, also, all my genuine friends who have kept me happy throughout the many years of my single life. This is my opportunity also to thank you for sharing in my happiness in finding John, and for all your thoughtfulness in so many ways.

Old Father Time, I thank you as well, but please keep your nose out of things now. John and I want to savour our life, not have it hurried on.

Thank you, everyone, for joining our celebration, and for all your kind wishes.

Appendix

Some useful addresses
Council of Churches of Britain and Ireland (CCBI), Inter-Church
House, 35-41 Lower Marsh, Waterloo, London, SE1 7RL.
Tel: 0171 620 4444.

Church of England:
The Faculty Office, 1 The Sanctuary, Westminster, London,
SW1P 3JT.
Tel: 0171 222 5881.

Enquiry Centre, Church House, Great Smith Street, London,
SW1P 3NZ.
Tel: 0171 222 9011.

Roman Catholic Church:
Marriage Care, Clitherow House, 1 Blythe Mews, Blythe Road,
London, W14 0NW.
Tel: 0171 371 1341.

Free Churches:
Free Church Federal Council (FCFC), 27 Tavistock Square,
London, WC1H 9HH.
Tel: 0171 387 8413.

Baptist Union, Baptist House, 129 Broadway, Didcot, OX11 8RT.
Tel: 01235 512077.

Methodist Church Office, 25 Marylebone Road, London, NW1 5JR.
Tel: 0171 486 5502.

The United Reformed Church, 86 Tavistock Place, London, WC1H 9RT.
Tel: 0171 916 2020.

Quakers:
Religious Society of Friends, Friends House, 173-177 Euston Road, London, NW1 2BJ.
Tel: 0171 387 3601.

Jewish religion:
Jewish Marriage Council, 23 Ravenshurst Avenue, London, NW4 4EL.

Marriage Authorisation Office, 735 High Road, London, N12 0US.
Tel: 0181 343 6301.
(Office hours: Sunday-Thursday, 10:30am-12:30pm)

General Register Offices:
General Register Office, Smedley Hydro, Trafalgar Road, Birkdale, Southport, PR8 2HH.
Tel: 01704 569824.

General Register Office for Scotland, New Register House, Edinburgh, EH1 3YT.
Tel: 0131 334 0380.

General Register Office, 49-55 Chichester Street, Belfast, BT1 4HL.
Tel: 01232 235211.